Praise for *Unlikely*

"I've known Kevin Palau for a few years now—not only is he one of the nicest guys I've ever met, but I've been amazed by how God has gifted him to really build the body and to bring a sense of unity to the church."

—Francis Chan

"Kevin Palau is a leader who 'has eyes to see' a vision for the future and 'ears to hear' rumblings of the Kingdom. But more than that, Kevin continues to be a vision-caster and rumbling-maker for the Church. In *Unlikely*, Kevin challenges dusty models of evangelism and helps a new generation dream about how the gospel might go forward in our day. You hold in your hands a book of hysterical hope and enormous courage, riddled with stories of transformative grace. I dare you to read it while sitting still."

—Jonathan Merritt, author of *Jesus Is Better Than You Imagined* and senior columnist for Religion News Service

"I am encouraged by the work of CityServe and the Luis Palau Association to bring churches together. This is a visual demonstration of the movement of the gospel in our city."

—Timothy Keller, bestselling author and pastor of Redeemer Presbyterian Church (NYC)

"Kevin Palau is a leader with a gentle spirit and a humble heart. He has a vision for what unites and not divides people and for how sincere followers of Jesus can best contribute to that. He lives what he speaks."

—John Ortberg, senior pastor of Menlo Park Presbyterian Church and author of *All the Places to Go*

"This book is a timely reminder that engaging culture, loving your neighbor, and serving those in need still resonate. Kevin Palau and the Palau Association have impacted millions around the world for many years while, just as importantly, making a difference and impacting the city of Portland. A great model for pastors, leaders and churches to love those around us. Read this book and you too will be inspired to be a world changer by simply impacting those closest to you in your city."

—Brad Lomenick, author of *The Catalyst Leader* and *H3 Leadership* and the former president of Catalyst

"I have a long list of people who I want to read this book. Kevin shares a mesmerizing, convicting, and empowering story of what can happen when churches unite to serve a city with no strings attached. I want this for my city. I want this for your city. I want this for every city."

—Kara Powell, PhD, executive director of Fuller Youth Institute, Fuller Theological Seminar

"Kevin has been a great inspiration in my life and work. His posture of humility combined with bold willingness to ask 'why not?' has forged unlikely relationships and renewal in some of the least expected places. I couldn't recommend his story highly enough."

—Gabe Lyons, Q Founder and author of *The Next Christians*

"As close personal friends with Kevin and the Palau Family, I can assure you, in them, there is only a passion to creatively find ways to deliver the Gospel Message in our ever evolving culture. The city movement is maybe the greatest model of revival at work today. It is bringing us to the heart of Christian faith, to demonstrate the love of Christ in our land."

—Pat Gelsinger, CEO of VMware

"Instead of getting mad about the secularizing changes happening in our culture and the people who embody them, Kevin Palau takes a different approach: he engages those people, forms friendships and partnerships with them, and join forces with them to serve others in need. If this is not what you expect from an evangelical Christian—someone in the family business of mass evangelism, no less!—take note. It's Christ-like, it works, and it's a major way forward in our changed 'post-Christian' times. Kevin spells it out nicely in this enjoyable and highly instructive book."

—Tom Krattenmaker, *USA Today* contributing columnist and author of *The Evangelicals You Don't Know*

unlikely

Setting Aside Our Differences to Live Out the Gospel

KEVIN PALAU

HOWARD BOOKS

An Imprint of Simon & Schuster, Inc.

New York   Nashville   London   Toronto   Sydney   New Delhi

Howard Books
An Imprint of Simon & Schuster, Inc.
1230 Avenue of the Americas
New York, NY 10020

First Howard Books hardcover edition June 2015

HOWARD and colophon are trademarks of Simon & Schuster, Inc.

For information about special discounts for bulk purchases, please contact Simon & Schuster Special Sales at 1-866-506-1949 or business@simonandschuster.com.

The Simon & Schuster Speakers Bureau can bring authors to your live event. For more information or to book an event, contact the Simon & Schuster Speakers Bureau at 1-866-248-3049 or visit our website at www.simonspeakers.com.

Interior design by Robert E. Ettlin

Manufactured in the United States of America

10 9 8 7 6 5 4 3 2

Library of Congress Cataloging-in-Publication Data is available.

ISBN 978-1-4767-8944-6
ISBN 978-1-4767-8945-3 (ebook)

With undying thanks to the pastors and leaders of the Portland area who have sought the "peace and prosperity" of the region so tirelessly.

Mom and Dad, thank you for modeling Christ-like love and a passion for the gospel.

Michelle, your love and patience are the fuel that keeps our family going. I love you.

David, Daniel, and Lauren, I'm so proud of you.

Keith, Andrew, and Steve, growing up and working with my brothers is an undeserved joy.

Contents

Foreword by Sam Adams, former mayor of the City of Portland

When Kevin and his dad, along with a handful of evangelical pastors, asked to meet with me about how they wanted to help in our public schools, I still remember thinking to myself, *They want my support for them to do* what?!

It was 2008. I was a newly elected progressive mayor of a very liberal city. An openly gay mayor at that! Growing up in Oregon, my experience with evangelicals was mostly negative. Based on my direct experience and what the mass media portrayed, I assumed most evangelicals were judgmental, accusatory, closed off, and unwelcoming.

I thought Kevin, his dad, and the evangelical pastors asking to meet with me had their presuppositions about me as well—that their request was a check-the-box official courtesy for whoever happened to be mayor.

I was weary, yes. Still, I hoped for something different. Dr. Palau and his team had a solid reputation. He was known as a passionate evangelist and faith community leader, but one who largely stayed outside of politics. I did not know Kevin.

As you will read, that meeting went much better than we each thought it would . . . thankfully.

Circumstances pushed me to listen with very open ears. We

were in the midst of a debilitating economic recession. Requests for city services were ballooning, while dwindling revenues required us to make cuts in our budgets. Deep cuts.

Kevin and the others came with a new kind of offer to help Portland. And their attitude was not at all what I expected. They were humble, not judgmental. They were open, not closed off. They wanted to work together, look beyond our differences, and serve the city. They made it clear that they had no hidden agendas. They offered humble community service, not self-promotion or inappropriate proselytizing.

And they delivered. Again. And again.

I so appreciate Kevin Palau and his leadership of the CityServe effort. CityServe Portland has done serious and important work in our city. The faith community has accomplished so much—in liberal Portland of all places! And I know it never would have happened if they hadn't approached us first. They took the first step. They made the first move. That says a lot.

This entire process has been very enriching for me personally as well. I have come to see the evangelical community more clearly. I have learned that many of my initial opinions were outdated, based on a narrow stereotype. Nothing showed me their compassion and grace more than when I found myself in the midst of a personal political scandal in 2008. They were dark days for me. I had made a big mistake. When some from my own community turned their backs on me, Luis and Kevin reached out. Luis met with me personally, prayed for me, and offered wise counsel. I'll never forget that conversation.

Over the years, as Kevin and the team have expanded to help other cities in similar efforts, I have received calls from other mayors (mostly from other big liberal cities). The question is always the same: "Did you really partner with the evangelical community?"

My response: "Yes, and we're better for it!"

I'm so glad Kevin wrote this book. I hope it encourages more individuals—more cities—to take on similar efforts.

Some who read this book might get riled up that Kevin, Luis, and other evangelical leaders crossed the ideological aisle, shook hands, started a conversation, and took action with individuals of different perspectives, faiths, and lifestyles. They might worry that Kevin and others have lost their edge, given in to cultural pressures, or forgotten what they stood for. I face similar questions from some of my own supporters.

I can tell you rather bluntly that Kevin has not lost his evangelical edge. I know where he stands. He, his dad, and the evangelicals in Portland love to share the message of Christ and aren't shy about it. Personally, I have not lost my progressive political outlook either. We still have different views on many issues. As one reporter put it, "These aren't petty disagreements."

But what has changed over the past several years—for Kevin and me and thousands of others involved in efforts to serve the city—is the realization that a life, a city, or a nation where partnerships can only happen when those involved have near total agreement on all issues, is a mistake . . . for all of us.

We need to learn to disagree in a civil manner. To share our beliefs and convictions with humble attitudes and hearts. We should always be looking for points of agreement, acting upon those points of agreement for the good of our society and culture. Anything less is a choice of our own making . . . a bad choice.

The partnership to serve our city has changed our city. It has changed me and the lives of countless others.

Foreword by Rick McKinley,
lead pastor at Imago Dei Community

I have been fortunate enough to work in many different denominational settings over the years. Whether it was small, rural-town America or in the urban core of a major city, I've been able to see "church" in several contexts. And that has shaped my ecclesiology—what Scripture defines the church to be rather than what culture expects it to be.

Knowing that the church exists for the sake of the world and not for itself—which is the picture Scripture gives us—we should be a benefit to the city. As Jesus taught, we are sent out into the world to be a blessing—to be a light in the darkness. But what does that look like? For a long time, I dug through Scripture trying to find the places where Jesus taught people how to evangelize, how to be on mission, how to serve their neighbor, how to "be the church." What I learned is that Jesus doesn't really ever teach a specific way to be the church. He challenges. He encounters. He disciples. He sends. He empowers. But essentially, people learn by simply being with him and watching him. He leaves it up to individuals and communities to figure out what it looks like in their contexts.

When I first came to Portland in 2000, I had a dream of planting a church in the urban core. I felt a lot of conviction around the idea of *being* the church instead of trying to *build* a church, and that dictated a lot of the decisions we made in the early years. (It still does today.) For me, that reality started with one question I heard someone kicking around: *If we ever left, would anyone notice? Would anyone care?* I think that's a question we all need to ask ourselves every once in a while.

Deep down, I wonder if we don't regularly engage with our neighbors, because, in reality, we don't *want* to engage with our neighbors. And that's a scary place to be. It's not a lack of information, but more a lack of formation.

We've come a long way. Not just our church or a handful of churches, but a major portion of the evangelical community in Portland. We have learned what it looks like to humbly step up and play a significant role in the city. A role that I believe would be missed if we ever stepped away. What I love about CityServe and the work that Kevin and I and dozens of other pastors and church leaders have helped establish in Portland, that it has rekindled our passion to serve, to share the Good News, to set aside our differences, and to love our neighbors as a collective community of Jesus-followers.

But hearts don't change through programs and efforts to serve the community alone. Hearts change when we get them in front of the living God who loves them. Lives change when God begins to shape them. And that's what we're seeing in Portland. As we serve, we are not only meeting the needs of our community, but we are showing a better picture of who God is. We are telling people a better narrative—that God and his followers care for them, are concerned for them, want to see them succeed and thrive, not only now but also in the age to come.

We all need redemption. Each one of us. And that's what this book, this journey, and this effort is all about. Redeeming the story of hurt and broken people. Being the church. Not building our own kingdoms. Not pushing our own agenda. Simply serving our neighbors and sharing the Good News, no matter their background.

This book might make you uncomfortable at times. That's a good thing. Kevin will be the first to admit he doesn't have it all figured out. It's a journey for all of us. We make mistakes along the way. But one thing I do know—the evangelical churches in Portland are looked at differently today than they were ten years ago. We are no longer seen as a judgmental and exclusive group. Instead, we are seen as an added resource and a blessing to our city.

Tremendous doors have opened for ministry and will continue to open. A vast amount of good, in the name of Christ, has been accomplished. New relationships have given birth to new endeavors. New churches are being planted and a gospel movement is flourishing. We are so thankful, because at the end of the day we want to see more people come to an understanding of the Good News of Jesus Christ. And because, at our core, we love our Lord and we love our neighbors.

Introduction

Good News in Portlandia:

An Unlikely Story

For I am not ashamed of the gospel, because it is the power of God that brings salvation to everyone who believes.

—Romans 1:16

I live in a town where 8,000 citizens cycle naked through the streets to remind the community of the impact of cycling on the environment and traffic. No one bats an eye, not even the police. The mayor simply tells them, "Be safe out there. Please wear shoes and a helmet."

When I tell people where I'm from, they'll sometimes launch into some lines from the hit IFC show *Portlandia*, which is spot-on in pointing out some of the quirky things that make Portland, Oregon, so lovably weird. (Yes, some people here may check a chicken's profile before they eat it, much like the characters from Season 1 of the popular comedy. "I guess I do have a question about the chicken," you might overhear in a restaurant in Southeast Portland. "If you can just tell us a little more about it? Is that USDA Organic, or Oregon Organic, or Portland Organic?" "The chicken you'll be enjoying tonight . . . his name is Colin. Here are his papers.")

In Portland, soccer rules. Ask anyone from the Timbers Army, the best supporters group in Major League Soccer. Every match is a sellout. But then again, Oregon Duck football rules, too. (They're the best team Nike can outfit!)

Beards, too. They're everywhere. And not just any beards. Real, grizzly man beards. The scruffier, the better.

You like beer? Portland is home to more microbreweries than any other city in the world. Or maybe coffee? It's one of the best cities in the nation—possibly the world—for coffee connoisseurs. (I can't touch the stuff, though. I'm wired enough as it is.) It's also a Mecca for foodies, full of cutting-edge restaurants and food carts galore. And I'm not sure, but is flannel still "in" throughout the rest of the country? If you're not wearing flannel in Portland, then you're probably covered in tattoo sleeves. We're the fifth most tattooed city in the United States.

Think it's something in the water? Not possible. We're the only major U.S. city left that refuses to fluoridate our water. It was actually a major political battle a few years back.

But it's not all tattoos and microbrews. Portland is buzzing with life and creativity. It is an energetic city full of culture and art and beauty and adventure. Our urban planning is forward-thinking and eco-commuter-friendly. Nothing beats our light rail system or our revitalized Pearl District. Too much of a loner for public transit? No worries. We have one of the strongest biking cultures in the nation. And here, fixies (aka: fixed-gear bikes) are king.

"But what about the rain?" some will ask. A true Portlander scoffs at the rain and doesn't even own an umbrella. We embrace that which makes this such an amazingly green place.

For all those reasons and more, Portland is full of young

people—young families, college kids, twenty-somethings—from all walks of life, and people are moving to Portland in droves. It was pioneers who settled this area, making the trek along the Oregon Trail. And pioneers are the ones who continue to make it their home today, individuals ready to take on the world, to take risks, and to have fun in the process. Sure, it's weird. We pride ourselves on that. (In fact, "Keep Portland Weird" is a popular bumper sticker. Whether or not Austin, Texas, came up with that first is a matter of debate.) But it's *our* weird city.

I'm lucky, I guess. I've always known and loved the Portland area. My brothers and I grew up here. My dad's an international evangelist from Argentina. He met my mom here when they were both attending Multnomah Bible College (now Multnomah University) in the early 1960s. They fell in love and stayed, even though my dad's work took him to Latin America and around the world on a regular basis. No strategy. It just made sense . . . well, as much sense as love can make for any of us.

Sometimes people ask me, "What's it like being a Christian in Portland? It must be hard living in such a liberal city." It's a fair question, I guess. After all, the *Huffington Post* says Portland's the least Christian city in the United States. (Do we get an award for that?) It's no surprise really. We have Reed College, dubbed the most liberal college in the country. We also had the nation's first openly gay mayor of a top-20 U.S. city, my friend Sam Adams. And then again, there are the naked bike riders.

The fact is, I love the diverse and free-spirited nature of Portland. I love the honesty and openness, the willingness to dialogue about any topic, whether the fluoride in our water, the number of bike lanes on our streets, or the God we attempt to serve.

If I answer the "What's it like being a Christian in Portland?"

question honestly, I would say it's like being home. Like all of us, I make my home in my community: where my kids go to school and where I work. There are, of course, things I would rather do without; it's true for any of us. There are also things I love. As a Christian, I find it doesn't help to rail against the context in which you live. Jesus called us to be a light shining on a hill. I don't know about you, but I can't shine if I'm always down on my own community.

What if we, as Christians, acted more out of love than out of anger? What if our message became less strident and more alluring? What if we worked with our fellow citizens and neighbors—even those we don't agree with on important issues—to accomplish something truly beneficial for everyone? And what if we accomplished all this *while* we joyfully and boldly shared the greatest news we've ever heard—the Good News of Jesus Christ?

That's my hope for every follower of Christ—to engage culture, not fear it. To love our neighbors, not condemn them. To serve those in need, not shy away from them. And to do it all boldly in the name of Jesus Christ.

What's it like being a Christian in Portland? It's grand and tough and nuanced and beautiful.

I believe Jesus wants us to be his light in any and all contexts, not just the ones in which we're most comfortable.

———

**Jesus wants us to be
his light in any and all
contexts, not just the
ones in which we're most
comfortable.**

———

Unlikely Friendships

I mentioned my friend Sam Adams, former mayor of Portland. We weren't always friends. We clearly don't come from the same background. Sam grew up on the rugged Oregon coast in a blue-collar family. He and his dad, a special education teacher and commercial fisherman, were never close. Sam's dad lost almost everything when El Niño moved the fish too far offshore for his 33-foot wooden trawler to reach. After his parents divorced, Sam and his mom did what they could to make ends meet. They survived for a time on food stamps and housing assistance, then eventually made their way to Eugene. Sam lived on his own from the age of fifteen, finishing high school and working hard to pay his way through four years at the University of Oregon.

Sam was already well into his career as a politician when he was "outed" by *Willamette Week*, Portland's alternative newspaper. Coming from a family of tough Montanans where there's a premium on being rugged and strong, being gay wasn't looked upon positively. Yet, in progressive Portland, he easily found community and family.

As I said, not quite the same backgrounds. Sam often says, "Our disagreements and differences are not lost on either of us."

My friendship with Sam represents part of my journey in life: learning to better understand and love those with whom I may not always see eye-to-eye on many issues.

The first time Sam and I met was in 2007. He was a city commissioner—one of five elected leaders overseeing the day-to-day operations of the City of Portland. A few dozen key Portland area pastors gathered with my dad and me to ask one question: How can we better serve the city and share the Good News? We had held some large-scale outreach festivals in previous years that drew tens of thousands to Waterfront Park to listen to great music and hear Dad share the Good News. They were powerful events, and we longed for even more impact. As we worked in the city, met with leaders, and talked with those who didn't share our faith, we recognized we had a major hurdle to overcome: when people heard the word "Christian," often what came to mind was less than savory.

A simple idea developed among many of the pastors. What if we went to see the mayor (at that time, our former police chief, Tom Potter) to ask a few simple questions: What are your greatest needs? How can we serve you? What if we could mobilize 15,000 volunteers to love and serve the city?

I'd just read the book *unChristian* by my friends Dave Kinnaman and Gabe Lyons. Sadly, it validated the reality we all were feeling. In the last few decades Christians have become more known for what we're against than what we're for. We've become thought of as an angry, defensive bunch. What two words best identified us in the minds of millennials (according to Dave and Gabe's research)? "Homophobic" and "hypocritical." Ouch.

Whether we thought this was fair or not, we felt we had to find ways to get beyond these tired labels to build relationships of genuine love and mutual respect with those we might disagree with, for the sake of the city and the sake of the gospel.

If evangelical Christian churches could unite and serve the community by opening more hearts to the gospel, I was in. More than that, I'd help organize it with our city officials.

Mayor Potter and other city officials, including then city commissioner Sam Adams, were a little taken aback by the meeting, and rightfully so. They assumed there was an agenda—some hidden motive. It only highlighted the clear divide between us that much more. Eventually, though, through multiple conversations, we were able to build trust, and together we identified five initial areas of need: hunger, homelessness, health care, the environment, and public schools. Our officials were thrilled to receive the assistance, and so began an unlikely partnership between the City of Portland and a growing band of churches.

Amazingly, the partnership not only worked, it blew everyone away, including us. And it continues to thrive today. What began as an honest effort to assist the community turned into a recurring relational movement of thousands of Christ-followers working together to seek the peace and prosperity of the city—hand-in-hand with anyone who shared the vision of a Portland where more and more could experience the sort of life God intended. It turned into an effort we now call CityServe.

In a fresh way, I found myself feeling proud to be a follower of Jesus in Portland.

It was something seemingly new and different, yet not so different at all. We were simply recovering truly biblical ways of living, loving each other as brothers and sisters in Christ and reflecting the Good News to our friends and neighbors. As we did this, we were following in the footsteps of Jesus and the early church, playing our small part in the unlikely movement Jesus began—the gospel movement.

A Rich Heritage

As I now find myself sitting across the table from civic leaders around the country, trying to explain what has happened in Portland and what is possible in their cities, I often start with a simple question: "Would it help if I tried to explain what an evangelical Christian actually is?"

The typical response is a look of relief. "That would be great!"

Many intelligent folks outside of our community struggle to make sense of it all, especially due to media portrayals and misconceptions. I find myself joyfully explaining the fact that in spite of many differences among Christ-followers, we represent by far the most diverse community out there—a 2,000-year-old movement that is found in every corner of the world, with people speaking virtually every language and representing every segment of society and socioeconomic level. We are a group united by the belief that our lives have been radically transformed by a person who lived thousands of years ago, and whose presence in our lives today leads us to love and serve our communities and to try our best to share this message of hope with everyone we can.

We are—or should be—a group of people radically transformed and yet, if we're honest, still radically broken. We are a people in whom Jesus himself, by his Spirit, actually lives!

———

We are—or should be—a group
of people radically transformed
and yet still radically broken.

———

How can we best demonstrate—to ourselves and to others— that Jesus lives? The evidence is spelled out by the Apostle Paul: "The fruit (evidence) of the Holy Spirit is this: Love, joy, peace, patience, kindness, goodness, faithfulness, gentleness, and self-control" (Galatians 5:22). Imagine the impact of a community where those things are the norm! Where that is what we are known for! That sounds like a movement that can't fail, that can't help but have an impact. An unlikely movement of unlikely people changing the world in unlikely ways. The same power that raised Jesus from the dead, Paul explains in Romans 8, is now resident in us.

When I think about the gospel, I think about it in terms of the tangible impact it has had on the community of Portland. The impact of schools and kids in foster care being loved and served. The impact of people hearing and responding to the Good News. That impact has inspired many other parts of the country. Towns and cities and suburbs are seeing what can happen if we uphold common causes and care for one another and share the message of Jesus. As a Christian, I am compelled by this, not only from a common-good-for-humanity perspective, but also from a good-for-eternity perspective. Both have to be considered and pursued in our ongoing cultural engagement. When we fail to carry both perspectives, we do the gospel a disservice.

I like to put it this way: we are wildly enthusiastic about loving and serving our neighbors, and we are wildly enthusiastic about sharing this message of Good News. Both are essential, and each can enhance the other.

I think it's easy to forget how impactful the gospel can be—how far it can penetrate—when we look beyond our differences with one another and form genuine friendships with people who do not hold our values or faith. Friendships that allow people to see Jesus in us, broken as we are. Friendships that help people hear of the one who can rescue any of us. Who would have thought that Portland would emerge as an epicenter of faith and cultural engagement? Who would have thought that in this volatile culture of taboos and political correctness, an openly gay mayor and the head of a Christian evangelistic organization would find friendship and be able to work together to improve the community?

There's really nothing new under the sun. People with a passion to obey Christ, love their neighbors, and share the Good News have always tried to find fresh ways to live out and express the message of Christ. Times have changed. There is no arguing that. Our culture has shifted dramatically, and that can be profoundly disconcerting. But as long as there are others who need help—who need the hope of Christ—his followers should do their utmost to join in the public square, take up the cause of their fellow man (and woman), and humbly and joyfully reflect Christ the best we can, in both word and deed. We need to be pushed by the Spirit to places where we have no choice but to depend on God to give us what we need to survive. It quickens our hearts and pushes us beyond our own comfort. And it's only beyond our own comfort that we discover the joy of the gospel.

Unlikely Evangelists

For years I struggled with the word "evangelist." I believed wholeheartedly in the role, and still do. My dad is an evangelist. My younger brother Andrew is as well. I love what they do. I've given my life to it. Yet, growing up, the word "evangelist" was such a foreign concept outside the church.

Today, however, our world is full of evangelists. It's no longer a strange, archaic word, as multibillion-dollar tech companies like Instagram now hire community evangelists. Many Fortune 500 companies employ chief evangelists or brand evangelists. And most sixteen-year-olds don't know it, but they also play the role of evangelist for a number of companies—Apple, Nike, you name it. They believe so passionately in someone or something that they can't help but share it boldly with others.

That's my heart for all followers of Christ: that today's gospel witnesses may not only be evangelists on stage at a festival (as wonderful and necessary as I believe that to be), but would also be hundreds of churches and thousands of individual believers joining with others in the public square, serving with those of differing backgrounds, and feeling empowered to share the Good News naturally, boldly, and lovingly.

My hope is that this book will open up some fresh vistas on how God can use any of us, unlikely as it might seem, to propel the kingdom forward in our communities, as we love each other, serve humbly, and joyfully tell the story of a God who has changed our lives.

Chapter One

Something Old, Something New:

An Unlikely Background

"For I am about to do something new.
See, I have already begun! Do you not see it?"
—Isaiah 43:19 NLT

There Dad stood, more than forty years ago, in the middle of the bullring with his black slacks, black suit coat, white shirt, and black tie. Black Ray-Ban sunglasses to shield his eyes from the blazing sun. He stood, looking a little like Johnny Cash, only he wasn't growling out "Ring of Fire." He was holding up his Bible in one hand, the other hand raised to the sky. The sun beat down as his voice rang out to the captivated audience in Quito, Ecuador.

To Dad, bullring or flatbed truck or packed arena, it didn't matter. His love was Jesus Christ and the life-changing Good News he brings. All these years later when I think about the early days—before we moved back to Beaverton, a western suburb of Portland; when we were living in Costa Rica, Colombia, and Mexico—I think about the bullring. I think about the big posters all over town with my dad's smiling face on them. He was a big deal to some, but he was always just "Dad" to us. He was a husband, a father, a man who loved Jesus and wanted to tell as many people about him as possible. It was as simple as that.

From the time he was a kid, raised in a small village just outside Buenos Aires, Argentina, Dad had a heart to share the Good News he and his family had experienced.

Dad was only ten when his father died. Grandpa was thirty-four. He came down with bronchial pneumonia right in the midst of World War II (which meant there was no penicillin). Dad remembers getting the call from his aunt, telling him to rush home from the British boarding school he attended as soon as possible. His father didn't have much time left. The fever was eating him up.

By the time he got there, though, Grandpa was already gone, but the story Dad heard became seared into his mind. As Grandpa lay dying in bed, burning up from the fever, barely hanging on to life, he suddenly sat up and sang a Salvation Army song as he clapped his hands: "There's crowns up there, bright crowns for you and me." Then his head hit the pillow, and he pointed up to heaven and quoted St. Paul, saying, "I'm going to be with Jesus, which is better by far." Those were his final words.

That was it for Dad. Even at a young age, he knew. "I'm going to tell people about Jesus," he said. "I want everyone to have the hope my dad had, even in the midst of death."

Dad was relentless in his ministry. It started with small neighborhood meetings. Then he and his buddies bought a tent. They traveled the region during the summer, putting on outreach campaigns and gatherings. As soon as he gained momentum in the 1960s, he was off and running. People often called Dad the Billy

Graham of Latin America. Their ministries were similar. After all, Dad had the greatest respect for Mr. Graham and had spent years learning from him. It was Mr. Graham who gave the seed money for Dad to start his own ministry. It was Mr. Graham who opened doors for him in many places around the world. It was Mr. Graham who was always ready to give insight, encouragement, and wisdom when needed.

Adopting Billy Graham's crusade model, Dad introduced this style of mass evangelism to Latin America and was one of the first evangelists to develop a radio ministry across the continent. Today he continues his strong radio presence on over 2,600 stations throughout the region. It's one of the reasons he's so known and loved by millions down there. In fact, Dad will sometimes have leaders, even presidents, pull him aside and tell him, "You know, Palau, my mom made me listen to you every morning when I was a kid."

Dad was also one of the first to try live television. In cities where we hosted crusades, he would appear on television and open up the phone lines to counsel people about family problems, faith, you name it.

I remember going with him to the TV studios at HCJB in Quito, Ecuador. My twin brother, Keith, and I got to go in front of the cameras to invite the audience to come to the crusade each evening. We were two little blond boys, which in itself created a certain level of interest. In a place where everyone had jet-black hair, people would routinely come over to touch our white-blond hair. It's amazing what you get used to.

I never doubted Dad's methods. In fact, I felt proud of him and his commitment to God when I watched him in the bullring—the Johnny Cash evangelist—passionately imploring folks to come forward to receive Christ. It was Dad's desire to introduce all people to the Jesus he loved, and to whom he'd given his life and family and ministry.

Dad was not only a great dad; he provided a never-ending opportunity to travel around the globe, mostly around Latin America when we were kids and in Europe during our teen years. I remember the first time Dad took Keith and me to a crusade with him. It was in San José, Costa Rica. We must have been eight or so.

Those being simpler and safer times, Dad didn't seem to think it was much of a risk to leave us alone for parts of each day at the hotel to explore and swim while he'd be off meeting with the president, speaking to local business leaders, or preparing for that evening's rally in the local soccer stadium.

It was a thrill to attend the crusades in the evenings. I loved seeing thousands of people gathering each night, joyful to be together with brothers and sisters in Christ from many different churches, proud to be able to express their devotion, and eager to share the Good News with others.

The highlight of those nights was always when Dad would give the "invitation." It was the climax of the whole gathering, the time when everyone would be led in a simple prayer, opening their hearts to Christ in response to the biblical message. Following the prayer, Dad would issue a challenge for folks to leave their seats and make their way down to the front of the stage. The people who came forward were joined by local counselors, believers who'd been specially trained to answer questions and pray with those who were responding either for the first time or perhaps recommitting their lives to Christ after having drifted away over the years.

It was stunning to see God move in such a tangible way, seeing hundreds stream forward. And this is what the whole program was geared toward: the invitation.

When I look back on those times from my youth, I am filled with feelings of pride—pride for my dad and what he accomplished, but even more, how strong his heart was to do something few were doing—something so difficult—because he felt called by God.

Growing Up Palau

People sometimes ask me what it was like growing up as the son of such a well-known man—whether I felt the pressure to measure up or struggled living in the bright lights. In reality, it was a pretty normal life. For the most part, no one knew Luis Palau in Beaverton, Oregon. My childhood—aside from the occasional trip to Latin America for a crusade—involved the normal experiences of any suburban family.

Just because I grew up Palau didn't mean I inherited a faith in Christ. On the one hand, I'm guessing few people heard a clear expression of the gospel as often as my brothers and I did. I was one of those kids who prayed to receive Christ countless times, just to be safe. I can't point to any one time that I first committed my life to Christ. It was something I reconfirmed over and over in Sunday school classes in Mexico City and at Vacation Bible School.

For me, personally, I look back to when I was sixteen years old as the time when I made a more mature commitment to follow Jesus for the rest of my life. It was at a Christian camp and conference center called Hume Lake near Fresno, California. A speaker named Bill McKee challenged us to stand up in front of everyone if we were willing to share our faith and not be "lukewarm." As simple as it may seem now, it was a powerful moment for me. I felt convicted about certain things I was doing, music I was listening to, habits I was forming. I stood up in front of several hundred other kids, hands sweating, looking down at the ground, and felt a sense of relief that I was clear on my life's purpose: to do what I could to help lead people to Jesus.

It was a pivotal moment for me. I returned home with clarity and excitement. My brother and I became far more active in our church's high school group than we had been before. We even led Bible studies and prayer times at Sunset High School.

Just recently at one of my high school reunions (I won't tell you which one), Keith and I were surprised by the number of people who came up to us to tell us how much our actions played a role in their lives. One old friend told us, "You didn't know this at the time, but I saw you guys praying in the school library on a regular basis. God used that to plant some seeds in my life. I came to trust God in my twenties, and my wife and I now attend Village Baptist."

It is such a privilege even now to see how those personally monumental moments of childlike faith can be used by God in other people's lives.

The Winds of Change

During those early years of my commitment to Christ, I devoured books like *Shadow of the Almighty* by Elisabeth Elliot (as well as *The Lord of the Rings*, but that's another story). It was that book—a book about a missionary from Wheaton College who was martyred in Ecuador in the 1950s—that pushed me to attend Wheaton myself. (It didn't hurt that Billy Graham had gone there as well—Dad never let us forget that!) I loved my years as a Wheaton student. God used my time there to develop my Christian worldview and kindle the dream of how to live out the school's motto: "For Christ and his kingdom." I felt sure God wanted me to serve him in some way related to missions; I just wasn't sure exactly how.

The August after finishing my studies, Michelle and I got married. (We met in the youth group at Cedar Mill Bible Church, where we'd both grown up.) I started working for my dad that same month. It was only supposed to be for a year, just as we got settled into married life. A chance to pay off some student loans and get ready for Fuller Theological Seminary in Pasadena. I'd already been accepted. Seemed to have my trajectory figured out. But a funny thing happened in those first six months. I fell in love with the work, the joy of seeing dozens, even hundreds, of churches, working together to try to impact their cities. That resonated with me. I was hooked.

Plans quickly changed. Michelle and I knew we needed to stay on longer with the team. We bagged the Fuller Seminary plans and decided to dig our roots into Portland—the place we both loved.

I became the guy whose job it was to fly out to various U.S. and international cities to meet with pastors who wanted to have a Luis Palau Crusade. It was up to me to cast the vision of what this effort would do for their community and why it was worth the significant investment of time and money. I knew the routine. After all, I'd grown up in the midst of these crusades. I knew what they could do, and I believed in them wholeheartedly.

Some of the selling points, for lack of a better term, remain the same today: the value of uniting churches across denominations and ethnicities, equipping folks from those churches in sharing their faith in a visible, large-scale way. I was a pretty naïve twenty-two-year-old, fresh out of Wheaton College, when I started flying around to places like Kingston, Jamaica, and Manhattan—Kansas, that is—trying to lay the foundation for a successful crusade. I loved it, but bit by bit, I became aware of critiques of the crusade approach. Not everyone was as excited and convinced as I was. The pushback usually ran along certain lines:

- Are the crusades reaching those who need to hear the gospel, or are we preaching to the choir?

- Do the people who respond to the gospel message end up in local churches?

- What's left a year or even six months after you guys leave?

I had never really thought about the crusade approach in this way, this critically. For me, what made these critiques tough to stomach was that they came from the very people I was supposed to convince.

I developed my answers to these questions and critiques, but, over time, doubts began to gnaw away at me, especially when attendance at our U.S. events started to decline and costs climbed. Were there better ways to do this? If so, what were they, and where were the examples of these better approaches?

We, as a family and a team, felt the clear conviction that the best way to change a person's life for the better was to help them see and experience God's love by sharing the Good News with them. If there was a better way to impact a city and share the gospel, what was it?

Harder than I Thought

When I was thirty-two, "Say Yes, Chicago" came along. Michelle and I had started our family. David was four, and Daniel was just eighteen months old. Dad had long dreamed of tackling this big, tough city—"my kind of town," according to Frank Sinatra. We had a lot of good relationships from Wheaton College and Moody Bible Institute, and Dad had preached in Chicago many times over the years.

We thought this time we'd try something new. So, we embarked on a fresh (for us) approach. Really, it was an older approach: taking on a city for much longer than just a week. What evolved was the idea of doing what Billy Graham had done effectively in the 1950s, where, for example, he filled New York's Madison Square Garden for (if you can believe this) four months straight. That was in the summer of 1957. For Dad, as a twenty-three-year-old just getting geared up to move to the United States for further theological studies in Portland, Oregon, hearing and reading about that marathon crusade at Madison Square Garden was one of the primary things that cultivated his vision for this sort of big-city effort.

It wasn't completely new to us. In the past, we had tried it in other cities with varying success. "Mission to London" in 1984 was sixteen weeks long. It was challenging at times, but the fruit was clearly visible. Even today, many church leaders (like worship leader Matt Redman) look back to that campaign as the beginning of their walks with Christ.

Dad wanted to tackle Chicago by taking one venue and staying there for several months, but I felt that approach would lead to disaster. If we were struggling to fill an arena in the United States for five or eight days, how were we going to survive two months? We eventually compromised. I moved to Chicago with Michelle and the boys to settle in for a two-year time of preparing. It was grueling, traveling all over the Chicago area, visiting pastors from the North Shore to the South Side. Some loved our idea; more were unsure but polite. It takes something out of you to try to sell a vision day after day after day, knowing many people aren't buying it.

In the end, we pulled together a schedule that included two months of outreaches, ranging from women's luncheons to rallies in suburban arenas, to two weeks at the UIC (University of Illinois at Chicago) Pavilion. Over the course of those months, tens of thousands of people heard the Good News, and thousands committed or recommitted their lives to Christ. I truly am grateful to have been part of it all. But I had this sinking feeling that the ambivalence from many churches that had been masked fairly well in the suburbs would be uncovered in a very public way when we began our fourteen nights of outreach in much tougher urban Chicago.

I've always struggled with anxiety. I still deal with it today. Yet never have I felt so claustrophobic and sick as when dawn broke on the opening day at UIC Pavilion. (In writing this chapter I was surprised at the feelings it still brings up.) It was a Sunday. I felt I just couldn't face what I was convinced was going to be an unmitigated disaster. It was humiliating to call Dad and say I wasn't coming, after spending the better part of two years preparing for this—traveling all over trying to enthuse Christians to come with their family and friends. Dad was understanding and didn't push me, though I'm still embarrassed I didn't have the courage to go.

I paced around the small missionary apartment we'd been living in those two years, courtesy of our friends at Winnetka Bible Church, waiting for a phone call from one of the crusade staff. My heart sank when finally, around 9:30 P.M., I got a call with the news. Fewer than 2,000 people, in a venue that held 8,000.

My worst fears were confirmed. My work had been shown to be wanting. I felt like an utter failure. What made it even worse was that at the opening of the message, Dad had publicly said, "My son Kevin warned me this might happen."

I somehow braced myself and attended several of the remaining nights. It was a bit of a blur. I tried to smile and make small talk backstage beforehand with the various pastors and Christian leaders I'd worked side by side with for the past two years. I did my best to pretend I wasn't churning inside, wanting to sneak away the first chance I got. I mean, what could you do at that point? Magically make folks appear?

I remember resigning from the team several times during those weeks. Of course, it was only to Michelle. It didn't ever really get close to being put on paper. I loved and admired my dad all the more for his amazing love for Christ, the churches, and the people of Chicago that led him to mount that stage night after night to share the Good News of a God who loves us so much he was willing to do anything to draw us back into a relationship with himself.

Chicago was a turning point for me. I determined if we couldn't find another way to reach people, I'd have to consider quietly finding another way to serve God. Maybe I could finish my master's degree at Wheaton and teach?

An Aging Model

The old methods were not working as well as they used to, at least not for us, especially in the United States and other Western nations. It wasn't anyone's fault. I didn't hold my father, or other evangelists who utilized this approach, in any kind of contempt for it.

And some are still seeing wide success, which is wonderful. It just wasn't working for us.

I wanted to tell people about the relationship with God I had found as a young man. I wanted to show others the person of Christ, the person I saw in Dad and in Mom and in so many other leaders I had the privilege of meeting. And I knew I wasn't alone. All those leaders I met in Illinois and Jamaica and Kansas—the ones who gently raised questions about our methods and effectiveness—they weren't against the gospel. They weren't down on evangelism. They just had the same questions I did.

None of us have perfect childhoods, but I think sometimes we can be fortunate to be spared from certain things that might otherwise hobble us in our faith. Being the son of an evangelist had given me such a global view of the gospel and how that message could change a person's life and how that life could, then, change a whole community. I saw in our Chicago approach, though, a method that had, perhaps, run its course, at least in parts of the West. And one question haunted me:

Was there another way?

Was there a way to keep all the great stuff of the crusade approach, the model Billy Graham had used for decades that had found various sorts of expression for more than a hundred years through the likes of D. L. Moody, Billy Sunday, and others? Was there a way to build upon that foundation and move it forward? Certainly, we weren't the only ones asking these sorts of questions. Other great evangelists, like Greg Laurie, were building on the Graham model as well—focusing on great music, creative design, and the best in media to communicate the Good News more clearly. It seemed obvious to most of us that the culture was shifting. Was there a way to create a better environment for the powerful message of the Good

News, allowing it to be unleashed more naturally and empowering believers to live it out in their own lives on a daily basis?

As an association, we had never *really* practiced what we preached in our hometown of Portland. Over the years, the local churches had grown to love and trust Dad, as he'd spoken in most of the larger churches over the decades. The city had its own Billy Graham Crusade in 1992 at Civic Stadium (now Providence Park, where the Timbers play soccer). The Graham Crusade was a phenomenon. It overflowed the stadium into nearby Lincoln High School for eight days.

Five years later, those same pastors felt it was time to unite again to share the same message, and they wanted our team at the helm. I was determined to try something different. There was no way I wanted to do something that could be compared to Billy Graham's 50,000-plus attendance per night. And there was no way I was going to relive Chicago. I still remember talking about it with my younger brother Andrew and Dad in his kitchen.

"What if we put on a two-day music festival in a park? Bring in great bands, food, even corporate sponsors?"

To be honest, some of my stance was based on fear. If we did this outdoors at, say, Waterfront Park—the living room of the city, where thousands came for annual events—there would be no empty seats. Even if just 3,000 people came, they could spread out on blankets, and it wouldn't feel too bad. (Some faith and vision!)

But despite that, the kitchen vision caught on. Sometimes God uses even our lack of faith for his own ends.

———

**Sometimes God uses even our
lack of faith for his own ends.**

———

"Maybe with a family fun zone people could bring their little kids. They wouldn't need to find babysitters."

"Would folks be more likely to try bringing their friends who need to hear the message? It might be more comfortable for them if they can come and go as they please."

We talked and talked, and the idea grew and formed into something pretty interesting. When we pitched it to the pastors in our community, they seemed excited. And then, the typical year of behind-the-scenes preparation progressed. There did seem to be a fresh enthusiasm. In the back of my mind, I thought, *This might actually work!*

Still, when the festival week began, Dad was nervous.

"What have my sons gotten me into? What if this flops? We live here! What will my mother-in-law think?"

Dad was so nervous he decided to move into the Marriott Hotel downtown, just a block from Waterfront Park, along the Willamette River. He wanted to be able to pray and to get away from any distractions.

When the day actually came, I was amazed. People started to show up in droves, overflowing all the arrangements we'd made. It was by far the largest U.S. crowd we'd ever seen. A brand-new opening band that few had heard of called Skillet played, along with TobyMac and Kirk Franklin. It was a blast! People sat on blankets with friends and lined up to get ice cream, lemonade, burgers, and corn on the cob. The kids hung out and played in the Veggie Tales Family Fun Zone, or watched X Games–caliber athletes skate, including guys like Jamie Thomas. More important, of course, was the opportunity for the church to be visibly together in the heart of the city, worshiping together and sharing the life-changing message of Jesus.

It had felt risky. I mean, you can't really hide from a massive flop in your hometown. But, thank the Lord, and thanks to the amazing local churches that joined us in the risk, it wasn't a flop. It was a spark. A spark that launched a new model for evangelistic festivals around the United States and the world.

Seeing the Gospel

Invitations for Palau Festivals, as we now called them, came from Myrtle Beach to Houston, the Twin Cities to Ft. Lauderdale, San Diego to Washington, D.C. International cities such as Buenos Aires, Argentina; Newcastle, Australia; Tirana, Albania; Suva, Fiji; Madrid, Spain; Cairo, Egypt; Kigali, Rwanda; and beyond. Dozens of cities in all. They caught the vision, jumped on board, and saw great fruit. It really did feel like a breakthrough. And in a way, it was. This approach felt fresh. We were getting out closer to where folks lived and breathed. The festivals created a family-friendly, nonpolitical environment that blended a music festival with direct preaching. We met amazing friends along the way and had once-in-a-lifetime experiences.

The new model didn't come without its challenges. It was a little more complicated to figure out how to have folks respond to the gospel message, since there was no room for them to come forward for the invitation. As a result, we began training local followers of Christ as festival counselors to watch for the hands that would go up and approach individuals right there, in the midst of the crowd. It lacked a bit of the drama of the past, but it worked.

Still, as a few more years went by and the newness of the model wore off, some of the same questions remained:

- What really remained after we left town?

- Did the unity among the churches continue?

- How could it, when we'd left no clear means for that to happen?

- Were we even reaching the right audience, or just preaching to the choir?

I have always had a way of driving myself crazy that way. The questions. The doubts. But looking back, they seemed to be leading us somewhere. And it was only a matter of time before another little glimmer would shine. A way to build upon this festival model and make the fruit even more long-lasting. And funny enough, the next big breakthrough again came in good ol' Portland, among the least-churched and most progressive cities in the United States.

Attractional vs. Missional, and Other Loaded Words

As wonderful as the festivals were, and still are, they are examples of the attractional approach to ministry. In other words, "What can we do to create an attractive environment for people to come and hear the message?"

There's nothing wrong with that. We want to see more churches and ministries that are attractive and winsome. (After all, what's the alternative? The opposite of attractive is repulsive.) Yet, as many in the church were wondering, was there more to our witness than attractional ministry? Was it really just a matter of building bigger church buildings and having better worship bands and more exciting kids' programs? Of having better and better bands at festivals? Is that, in and of itself, enough? We all wondered if there was more we could do.

The word "missional" is admittedly in danger of growing stale from overuse. But to me, it still communicates that new/old vision of the early church—to be on mission with Christ. Isn't that our hope? For our communities? Our families? Our children? Ourselves? Unleashing more followers of Jesus to see their lives as a mission to love others and share the Good News?

My mind was spinning. How would communities respond to a kind of Christian witness that dug right into their own neighborhoods and truly helped—truly loved—because God so loved the world? In an oversaturated culture of rhetoric, could simple love in action prove to be a profound, ground-shaking witness? Could we recover a more radical expression of what Christians are to be known for on this earth?

If we, as Christians, are still known more for what we're against rather than what we're for, how likely is it that the people we are trying to reach will darken the doors of our churches or come to our festivals—no matter how great the coffee or how amazing the music? Some will always come. The gospel itself is attractive and relevant and powerful. Friends will invite friends, and neighbors will invite neighbors. That's always the core. And we must persist. But what else could we do to bridge the gap that seemed to be widening year by year, growing into a chasm that we could hardly see across?

The reality was that on a broader culture scale, at least in many parts of the United States, we had created our own Christian bubble. Our own music, books, video games, schools, churches. We had become experts at isolating and protecting ourselves from the very people Christ called us to love unconditionally.

Armed with a desire to get beyond the borders we'd set for ourselves and to see greater impact, seven years after the last festival in Portland, in 2007, we again gathered with dozens of key area pastors. We all agreed—we needed a fresh way to communicate the gospel that could fold into and enhance the festival model. It had to be sincere. It had to be relevant. But it also needed to be so much more than a method. It had to be a way of life. The idea was nothing new. It was biblical. It's the way the earliest followers of Jesus lived and shared the Good News.

Dale Ebel from Rolling Hills, a great suburban church, stood and told of the progress they'd been making in engaging the community, even taking a Sunday and canceling regular services to actually serve the community. It was like a lightbulb popped on.

The year before, at our Houston Festival, we'd been challenged by Jim Herrington, Dave Peterson, Rachel Quan, and many other great leaders there to think a little more creatively about a holistic "word and deed" approach to evangelism. That great challenge prompted us to organize a number of creative service projects there, partnering with local schools and meeting with the mayor to be sure he knew the festival was coming. But we knew we were just scratching the surface. Those conversations began to light a fire in my heart, as well as the hearts of many on the Palau Team staff.

It was simple, really. We wanted to add feet to our faith. The fact is, actions often speak louder than words. We needed to marry our words and our actions.

That afternoon at our Beaverton headquarters, we got excited at the thought of mixing things up. It was time for something a little different. The ideas began to swirl. Would a stronger and more sustainable commitment to serving the community find traction with the churches? Would local officials be open to some sort of partnership? Would this approach make the festival more effective overall? Would believers find better relational bridges to their neighbors if they served alongside them, showing unconditional love? Could the church, too often known for being hypocritical, angry, judgmental, and harsh, show a more Christ-like face?

Thus began a journey that would lead—through dozens of twists and turns—to unlikely opportunities and impact. It would include a unique chance to address dozens of individuals at the Q Center, Portland's LGBTQ community center, sharing my heart and hope for our city and speaking of the love of Jesus Christ. It would involve standing with our school superintendent in front of dozens of principals and pastors, forging new partnerships for the sake of our students. It would help develop fifteen free neighborhood medical and dental clinics run by area churches. A cover story in *Willamette Week* would end up praising the new effort by churches, an unprecedented move by the ultraprogressive media outlet. It helped launch the festival forward, gathering tens of thousands of people over two days at Waterfront Park in the summer of 2008 to hear the Good News presented by Dad and celebrate the work that was accomplished. These surprising open doors would be a glimpse of God's Spirit at work, and it's been a thrill. But the best part—the real foundation of it all—has been our recovering a confidence in the simple power of the gospel: lived out and proclaimed.

The True Source of Inspiration and Power

My dad's favorite Bible verse is Galatians 2:20. I've heard him preach about it on countless occasions:

> *I have been crucified with Christ and I no longer live, but Christ lives in me. The life I now live in the body, I live by faith in the Son of God, who loved me and gave himself for me.*

Most of us want to do something great in this world—to make a difference for our family, our children, or our community. We want to do our part. But what's enough? What's expected? What's even possible?

My dad was asking the same question in college years ago. He had just arrived in Portland from his home country of Argentina. He was fluent in English and Spanish—successful in the world's terms, as well as in spiritual terms. He had been on the radio for years, had spoken in dozens of churches, was being mentored by some of the greatest leaders in the Christian world, and was dreaming of beginning his ministry career as a world evangelist. But on the inside, he was falling apart. He felt like everything was a show. That's when Major Ian Thomas spoke in chapel.

Major Thomas was the founder of the Torchbearers, the group that runs the Capernwray Bible School in England. His thick British accent and frequent gesturing with a finger that had been partially cut off grabbed Dad's attention.

His theme was "Any old bush will do, as long as God is in the bush." It was based on the story of Moses and his encounter with God in the burning bush. It took Moses forty years in the wilderness to realize that he was nothing without God, Major Thomas said.

God was trying to tell Moses, "I don't need a pretty bush or an educated bush or an eloquent bush. Any old bush will do, as long as I am in the bush. If I am going to use you, I am going to use you. It will not be you doing something for me, but me doing something through you."

———

Any bush will do, as long as God

is in the bush.

———

It's funny how a message like that can stay so clearly in your mind for years. I wasn't even there. Not even a blip on the radar. But Dad has told me the story so many times that I can picture the chapel, Major Thomas, and the finger. I can hear the words.

As we gathered with those pastors in 2007 to talk about what God could do in Portland, I was brought back to Major Thomas's words. We were all that bush: a useless bunch of dried-up sticks. We could do nothing for God. All our reading and serving and asking questions and trying to model ourselves after others was worthless. Everything was futile unless God was in the bush—unless we came to the end of ourselves.

The astonishing fact is that Jesus lives within every believer, and they become one in spirit. The apostle Paul described this as "the mystery that has been kept hidden for ages and generations, but is now disclosed to the saints. To them God has chosen to make known among the Gentiles the glorious riches of this mystery, which is Christ in you, the hope of glory" (Colossians 1:26–27).

Christ living in and through us, by the Holy Spirit, was the only way to effectively live and serve. That was the key. No need to impress others. We just had to allow Christ to live in and through us. It's a lesson I have personally had to learn on many occasions.

Through my struggles and doubts and fears, I have found myself not more "right" in my interpretation of the gospel but more humbled by it—more in love with it. More in love with the simplicity of it. I came to recognize that no program or method is the answer, but rather the Spirit of Jesus working through me, and you, and thousands of others who, imperfect as we are, choose to follow Jesus today. This is the foundation that allows us to build unlikely friendships and find common ground we haven't seen before. To see our schools and community impacted. To build solidarity within and among the churches. To be more joyfully bold in sharing the Good News.

And when we find ourselves allowing Christ to live and work through us, an odd thing happens. We find the gospel—alive—in us! We find it is "no longer I, but Christ."

Chapter Two

The Only Time We've Got:

An Unlikely Context

Let us overcome by our manner of living rather than by our words alone. For this is the main battle, this is the unanswerable argument, the argument from conduct.
—John Chrysostom, Early Church Father

Engage! It's the generational battle cry of millions of mostly younger evangelicals who are pushing against what they see as tired methods of the church and angry public rhetoric. Enough of one-party politics. Enough of singular issues that define the Christian cultural agenda.

Our American evangelical church stands conflicted on issues ranging from gay marriage to Christian feminism. Older churches look with suspicion at those they consider "emerging," while younger leaders dismiss those who don't yet get it. Our culture has certainly grown more secular and even hostile toward faith. And our evangelical community seems to be splintering. Some feel strongly that mobilizing politically to "take back America" is the priority, the only hope to gain back the ground we've lost on social issues. If we can put godly leaders in power, then perhaps things will change. Others blame the media—the films, television, and radio that glorify attitudes and values contrary to Scripture and the timeless values of the past. If we can create quality content with wholesome values, or at least keep our kids away from the worst of media, perhaps we'll have a chance. Many feel not only frustration but anger at the direction we're heading, and it's tempting to focus on who's to blame, whether the president, Hollywood, or churches and pastors that aren't doing more to fight back.

Another approach many have taken is to withdraw and create our own separate institutions to protect ourselves. Our own media, schools, books, and Christian communities. Sound familiar?

Are we still in a culture war? Should we be? Many certainly feel we are, and no doubt, there is a lot to be concerned about in our culture. But are the only options to fight or take flight? Keep up the angry rhetoric that many younger evangelicals have given up on, or withdraw into a safe Christian bubble?

The question a growing number of believers in Portland are asking ourselves is simple: How do we engage? Not if or when, but how? Will we act in a biblical manner? A Christ-like manner? A holistic manner? This, in my mind, is the real challenge we must face. It isn't easy. In fact, it might be the toughest thing we've ever done.

It's clear what's not working. But what guidance can we look to—biblically and historically—to help us find the right sort of posture to take in engaging with our culture, sharing the Good News, and impacting our communities?

Many other leaders in Portland and I have been encouraged

and inspired by three historical examples of cultural engagement: the Jewish community in exile in Babylon six hundred years before Christ (Jeremiah 29), the birth of the first community of Christ-followers on the day of Pentecost (Acts 2), and the example of the church in the first few centuries under the persecution of the Roman Empire. In all three cases the people of God lived in a position of weakness, not only politically, but in nearly every way possible. If we think we have cause for discouragement, we can take courage from our brothers and sisters from the past who lived in far more challenging times. They not only survived; they thrived and changed the world.

Exiles in Babylon: Seeking Shalom

Do you ever feel like an alien in a strange land? Does it feel like the ground—the cultural landscape—has shifted out from under you? The leaders of the people of Israel certainly did in 597 B.C. After being defeated by one of the strongest empires of the day, King Jehoiakim and all of Jerusalem could only watch as the Babylonians sacked the capital, desecrated and destroyed the temple, and carried the political and religious leaders of Judah back to Babylon in chains. This season in the life of the people of God is where we get the well-known Sunday school stories of Daniel, the lion's den, Shadrach, Meshach, and Abednego, and the infamous fiery furnace.

In the midst of Israel's humiliation and bewilderment, questioning how God could have allowed such a thing, God speaks to the prophet Jeremiah, who is still in Israel. He sends a letter to the exiled leaders far away. I can imagine the sort of message from God they would have dreamed of: "Sit tight. Deliverance is coming. I'll take care of those hated Babylonians. They'll get what's coming to them." Here's what they actually got:

> *Build houses and settle down; plant gardens and eat what they produce. Marry and have sons and daughters; find wives for your sons and give your daughters in marriage, so that they too may have sons and daughters. Increase in number there; do not decrease. Also, seek the peace and prosperity of the city to which I have carried you into exile. Pray to the Lord for it, because if it prospers, you too will prosper.*

> —*Jeremiah 29:5–7*

Imagine how well this must have been received! They were far out of their comfort zones in a situation where the normal response would surely have been to circle the wagons and hunker down—to pray for God's deliverance!

"How can we sing the songs of Zion in a strange land?" God's people cried. They were among their enemies. Among people who spoke a different language, ate different food, worshiped different gods, and lived by different values. Sound familiar? So much of what I read online from some of my brothers and sisters these days has the tone of exile. They feel that we don't belong here anymore, that our country has been taken away from us, that the values are all wrong. They long to escape.

Why would God give the people of Israel such a message? Because the reality was, they were going to be there for a while. In fact, they were to live in exile in Babylon for more than seventy years.

The command is to "seek the peace and prosperity of the city to which I have carried you into exile. . . ." The Hebrew word translated as "peace and prosperity" in that passage is actually the word "shalom." Modern English doesn't do it justice. It's a rich, vibrant word, filled with hope for every good thing in life. It's what you wish for your children. What you hope for your family. What you pray for when you think about your loved ones. I've often heard my dad describe shalom as every good thing you want for your son or daughter on their wedding day— love, peace, security, financial success, joy, happiness, friendships. It's all encapsulated in the word "shalom."

What a shocking message for these Jewish leaders as they sat in exile!

Can you imagine their reaction? Seek the good of Babylon? Seek the peace of our enemies? Seek the prosperity of those who took us into captivity? I wonder how many of us feel like we're in exile in our cities or neighborhoods, that we're surrounded by people who don't share our worldview or values. Perhaps even that we're surrounded by enemies. Yet this same message applies.

Jesus took it a step further. "Love your enemies! Do good to those who hate you" (Luke 6:27 NLT). This kind of radical love— this seeking the good of those who hate you, let alone those who stand for different values—is to be the hallmark of a true follower of Jesus. The hallmark of a community that claims to have been transformed from within by an encounter with God.

Notice also that it's God who takes responsibility for taking them into exile. He says to seek the shalom of the city to which "I've carried you into exile." God had a plan and a purpose. Do you believe God has a reason for your living where you do? Living in the apartment complex or neighborhood where you are? What sort of a difference would that make in our attitudes if we believed that?

There was a season in the late 1980s and early '90s in Oregon when conservative Christians were known primarily for fighting politically, especially in the early days of gay rights—specifically, in 1992's Ballot Measure 9. The measure denied the use of government monies or properties to "promote, encourage or facilitate homosexuality, pedophilia, sadism, or masochism." It's understandable that Bible-believing followers of Jesus would want to uphold biblical values, as we should. Unfortunately, though, the spokespeople for this particular measure raised funds and put their case forward in a way that could only be described as bitter and mean-spirited.

The church lost that fight in more ways than one. Not only did the measure not pass, but it also marked a pivotal point in our relationship with the very people we were trying to serve and share the Good News with. In the hearts and minds of many, we simply became known as a conservative political group. That kind of reputation set a dangerous precedent and isolated us from the majority in Oregon. It left us with less and less common ground from which to build relationships of love and trust. I'm not saying we should stay away from political action or engagement. It's a blessing and responsibility we have as citizens and a chance to influence our culture. I'm also not saying we should be embarrassed about what the Bible teaches. We should always stand behind our convictions. I'm simply pointing out the danger of having that be the *only* or primary way we're known—for political battling, and for doing so with a posture of hatred, anger, and fear, rather than our love.

When the crusade days in the United States had waned and we were eager to try something new, we realized this close identification with political hot buttons was a factor that required some reflection and rethinking. Billy Graham had always cautioned Dad to be careful about politics.

"Luis," he'd say, "remember, you're in the role of the evangelist. You need to share the gospel with Democrats *and* Republicans, conservatives *and* liberals. Don't let yourself be pulled into partisan politics that cut you and the message off from anyone."

At the press conference for the very first Portland Festival in 1999, Dad stood with former Senator Mark Hatfield, who served as one of the cochairs for the festival. Senator Hatfield was a living, breathing example of a Christian statesman who practiced what he preached over decades of service in the U.S. Senate. He was always clear and joyful in the expression of his faith and was willing to take unpopular stands, including being among the few to stand against U.S. engagement in Vietnam. That day, Senator Hatfield shared, "We've done an excellent job letting people know what we're against. This festival is about letting people know what we're for—helping people find new life in Jesus Christ. Helping love and serve people."

The senator's comments resonated with many pastors and believers. The tough question his words implied echoed in our minds long after the press conference: How do we let people know the many things we're *for*? How do we seek the peace and prosperity— the shalom—of the place where we find ourselves living, working, and recreating? How do we find common ground?

The answer? By joining hands with community leaders and our *literal* neighbors to build a healthy community, strong public schools, a safe and clean environment for everyone. And yes, in the gritty work of doing good for all, when the opportunity presented itself, of course, to share the possibility of a new, transformed life from the inside out as a result of a relationship with God through Jesus Christ.

We knew we needed to recognize our changing context—the shift in our culture. Whether we liked it or not, this was the reality we had to live in and deal with. We could, of course, retreat farther and farther back, into our own world of Christian schools, Christian media, and our own churches and relationships. That was a very real possibility and, to some degree, understandable. Like any concerned father, I love my kids and don't want them to swallow, in an uncritical way, all that the world has to offer—the deceit of advertising's messages that fulfillment is found in what we own or the superficial depictions of love and sexuality. And yet, we longed to see people come to faith in Christ. We longed to see genuine relationships cultivated with our neighbors. We longed to live in such a way that, like the early church, our lifestyle and radical love caused many to rethink life and truth and hope and peace. To do this, retreating wasn't an option.

The Birth of the Early Church

The Jews in Babylon were challenged to seek the peace and prosperity of their city even while in exile. Another great encouragement and example for us comes from the birth of the church, as described in Acts 2.

After Jesus's death, burial, and resurrection, he appeared to his disciples with final instructions. Forty days later, he ascended into heaven. We actually have only a few comments from Jesus during this time.

"You will receive power when the Holy Spirit comes upon you; and you will be my witnesses in Jerusalem, and in all Judea and Samaria, and to the ends of the earth" (Acts 1:8).

Portland, Oregon, would certainly have counted as "the ends of the earth" to that small band of Jewish followers of Jesus. They'd previously been commanded to "go into all the world and preach the Good News to all creation" (Mark 16:15). But first they waited.

For what? The power Jesus promised. The power of his very presence, living in them, by the Holy Spirit. Like the exiles in Babylon, this earliest band of believers was numerically weak. The passage in Acts describes only one hundred twenty gathered in that room. Think of it. After Jesus's three years of earthly ministry, where at times thousands had followed him to hear him teach and see him perform miracles, that's what was left. One hundred twenty men and women gathered in a room.

When the day of Pentecost came, they were all together in one place. Suddenly a sound like the blowing of a violent wind came from heaven and filled the whole house where they were sitting. They saw what seemed to be tongues of fire that separated and came to rest on each of them. All of them were filled with the Holy Spirit and began to speak in other tongues as the Spirit enabled them.

Now there were staying in Jerusalem God-fearing Jews from every nation under heaven. When they heard this sound, a crowd came together in bewilderment, because each one heard their own language being spoken! Amazed and perplexed, they asked one another, "What does this mean?"

Then Peter stood up with the Eleven, raised his voice and addressed the crowd: "Fellow Jews and all of you who live in Jerusalem, let me explain this to you; listen carefully to what I say . . . God has made this Jesus, whom you crucified, both Lord and Christ." With many other words he warned them; and he pleaded with them, "Save yourselves from this corrupt generation." Those who accepted his message were baptized, and about three thousand were added to their number that day.

—Acts 2:1–6, 12, 14, 36, 40–41

On that afternoon, the early church was born.

Have you ever stopped to ponder how incredibly unlikely it is that this movement should have succeeded? Or that we should be here at all, still following in the footsteps of someone who lived and died 2,000 years ago? The thought never fails to encourage me. It's a huge boost to my own faith. They had absolutely nothing that we'd consider essential today to launch a lasting movement.

Influence? None. A bunch of fishermen and generally uneducated people.

Political power? Nope, not a bit.

Money? None to speak of.

A worldwide network to start out? Not at all. They all came from one small corner of the world and spoke the same language.

Technology? No mass media or even a printed New Testament. Only their own verbal testimony, a few letters, and later on, some written accounts.

Transportation? Not unless you count a donkey (the Mercedes-Benz of the day, as my dad always says) and their own two feet.

How easy it would have been for them to lose focus and heart—to be distracted by their shortcomings—to think about their lack of money, power, influence, connections. Yet, instead, they believed and obeyed. And a movement began. It swept across the known world faster than anyone could have dreamed. We're the heirs of this very same movement, removed as we may feel at times!

How did that early church behave in relationship to their culture and community? What characterized these first Christian believers?

They devoted themselves to the apostles' teaching and to fellowship, to the breaking of bread and to prayer. Everyone was filled with awe at the many wonders and signs performed by the apostles. All the believers were together and had everything in common. They sold property and possessions to give to anyone who had need. Every day they continued to meet together in the temple courts. They broke bread in their homes and ate together with glad and sincere hearts, praising God and enjoying the favor of all the people. And the Lord added to their number daily those who were being saved.

—Acts 2:42–47

Wow! What an example for us today!

- They devoted themselves to God's word (the apostolic teaching).

- They gathered together for fellowship, worship, and prayer.

- They met together in each other's homes, building community and practicing hospitality.

- They were radically generous, even selling their property to support each other.

So what was the outcome of this sort of Spirit-led living? They enjoyed "the favor of all the people," and "the Lord added to their numbers daily those who were being saved." In other words: favor and fruit. The kind of goodwill and intrigue-creating living that could and should characterize our Christian communities today.

As I reflect on our Portland journey, I see the church behaving in some of these same ways. Loving and serving each other within the family of believers. Living lives of radical generosity. Praying together. Sharing the Good News with love and boldness. And we are also beginning to see the same sort of favor with our city leaders and the community as a whole. Even more, we're seeing churches grow as people are putting their trust in Christ and wanting to become part of a family.

The Early Church and the Roman Empire

In Portland we've realized that we have little ability to "win" politically. We have scant shared Christian background to build upon. In some ways, that's healthy. It shakes us out of our complacency and encourages a humble, servant attitude. It diminishes any sense of entitlement. The Christian community in Portland is pushed to think more like missionaries. To be united in building the kingdom and sharing the Gospel. The early church had to operate in much the same way.

Before Constantine paved the way for the Roman Empire becoming "Christianized" in A.D. 313 (a mixed blessing), the believers had no illusion of controlling things. Of being "in charge." You think we have it tough? Imagine life for our brothers and sisters in the Roman Empire who were persecuted and killed for attempting to consistently live out their creed: "Jesus is Lord." I have a hard time envisioning them whining and complaining about how they were being treated. They had no illusions that life would be easy. "In this world you will have trouble. But take heart! I have overcome the world," their master had promised (John 16:33). Instead, over and over we read of their courage and peace in the midst of persecution. The presence of Jesus himself, by his Spirit, in their lives.

The early church had no assumption of rights, yet their joy in the midst of the storm changed many hearts and minds and ultimately transformed the Roman Empire. What exactly was it that led to the fantastic growth of the early church during this time? What did Christianity offer its believers that made it worth social estrangement, hostility from neighbors, and possible persecution? Scholars have put forward a number of important factors. Top of the list? A clear sense of community; complete equality, no matter their background or social class; support for one another in the midst of struggle and distress; and unique breakthroughs in the educational system, rooted in their desire to be able to read and understand the Bible.[1]

———

The early church had no assumption of rights, yet their joy in the midst of the storm changed many hearts and minds and ultimately transformed the Roman Empire.

———

All they had was the real, living presence of Jesus Christ himself—living in them through the Holy Spirit, giving them what they needed to bear witness and radically love in ways the world could not explain.

Consider some of these fantastic quotes from followers of

Christ in the first centuries of the church as primers for our own thoughtful and active love:

> *Do we not dwell beside you, sharing your way of life, your dress, your habits and the same needs of life? We stay beside you in this world, making use of the forum, the provision-market, the bath, the booth, the workshop, the inn, the weekly market, and all other places of commerce. We sail with you, fight at your side, till the soil with you, and traffic with you; we likewise join our technical skill to that of others, and make our works public property for your use.*
>
> —*Tertullian, ca. A.D. 196*[2]

Common ground. The early church understood that we live in community with those who don't share our faith. That we need to seek common ground with everyone possible, to let them see and experience our community in action, our love for one another, our generosity in practical application.

The early church was also radical in their care for the marginalized and forgotten:

> *They love one another. They never fail to help widows; they save orphans from those who would hurt them. If they have something they give freely to the man who has nothing; if they see a stranger, they take him home, and are happy, as though he were a real brother.*
>
> —*Aristides, second century A.D.*[3]

Did you catch that? "As though he were a real brother." They simply took Christ's teaching to heart. The marginalized are our brothers and sisters! The church was radical in generosity, tireless in service, and joyful in suffering.

The fourth-century church historian Eusebius describes the unlikely behavior of the early Christians in a time of plagues:

> *The evidence of the Christians' zeal and piety was made clear to all the pagans. For example, they alone in such a catastrophic state of affairs gave practical evidence of their sympathy and philanthropy by works. All day long some of them would diligently persevere in performing the last offices for the dying and burying them (for there were countless numbers, and no one to look after them). While others gathered together in a single assemblage all who were afflicted by famine throughout the whole city, and would distribute bread to them all.*
>
> *—Eusebius, fourth century[4]*

In a time of plagues beyond our imagination (Did you see *World War Z*?), where 30, 40, even 50 percent of towns and villages would perish, it was those who claimed to follow Christ who not only didn't run, but buried the dead, knowing full well it could mean their own deaths. They may not have had our understanding of how germs and viruses spread, but they knew full well it was death to stay. And they stayed. And they cared for the sick. Christians and pagans alike. How do you explain that? These were people from all walks of life—rich, poor, slave, free. All loving and serving in radical ways together, as the body of Christ.

Can we cultivate a heart for our communities like those early followers? A heart that goes beyond calling out sin and decrying everything we're against? Glimpses of God at work in Portland give me hope!

The End of Christian Culture Wars

We need to recognize the cold, hard reality of where we stand today and face it with confidence in the gospel. To paraphrase Dickens, whether these are the best of times or the worst of times, it's the only time we've got. I'm convinced we will not impact our nation through rhetoric and culture wars alone.

I remember being in middle school when Jerry Falwell and the Moral Majority began, when President Jimmy Carter made headlines by announcing that he was a born-again Christian. In some ways, our evangelical subculture took its present form in those days. Contemporary Christian music began! (There were no Christian music stations when I was a kid.) When Dad gave Keith and me, thirteen-year-olds, a cassette tape of a sixteen-year-old singer named Amy Grant . . . wow! My first crush! The first (and only) concerts I ever went to in high school were The Imperials, Keith Green, and later Amy Grant. Those were the days of the creation of a very specific, separate subculture, with our own versions of rock and pop music, our own comic books (I loved the Christian versions of *Archie*!), and for many, our own political leaders and party. They were heady days when many truly felt the country was ours to be taken back and that clearly laying out the Christian roots of our nation would help others realize the error of their ways. We would remind everyone, with strong words and strong speeches, that the Bible is what made America great.

Keith and I were in a band in high school. We originally played Beatles' songs. I played drums (poorly); Keith played bass; Kirk, our friend from church youth group, played keyboards and rhythm guitar; and our other friend Kelly, who wasn't a believer, played lead guitar.

We never played more than a handful of shows (if you can call them that). They were mostly in our garage with the door open for a few neighborhood kids. Then, summer camp. The one where Keith and I stood and committed our lives to Jesus. We felt challenged by the speaker to stop listening to secular music. We destroyed our secular records, and that was that! Now what I wouldn't give to have those old Beatles records on my shelf!

We returned from camp and, with a mixture of boldness and embarrassment, told Kelly we couldn't play Beatles covers anymore. We could, however, play Christian rock. Kelly gave it a try for a few weeks and then passed me a note in U.S. history class that said he was done. I wasn't too surprised.

I was left with mixed feelings. Were we being righteous and standing up for the truth? Or, had we just ruined a friendship and a great opportunity to help Kelly better understand the love of God through Jesus Christ? We loved Kelly and wanted him to "repent and come to the knowledge of the truth." But what was the best way to go about it?

Who Repents First?

Sad to say we can often be our own worst enemies. We long to see people come to faith in Christ, for their own good, for the good of their families. To see them join a loving community that's making a difference. We know that the word "repent" isn't a bad word. It's a rich, biblical word that simply means to "turn around" or "change your mind." We've experienced the joy and new life that comes from turning around in this way. Those of us who claim to follow Jesus have repented, at least initially. We've agreed with Scripture's assessment of us, that we are beyond hope if left to our own devices. That even our well-meaning efforts fall far short. That our motives are so mixed and mixed up that only a radical in-breaking of God's love in the person of Jesus could ever redeem us. We know that and feel it.

Yet somehow when we ask others to repent, that doesn't come across. I think it's because they don't see us doing it first! I love the way my friend, Pastor Rick McKinley from Imago Dei Community in downtown Portland, puts it: "We need to preach the gospel to ourselves first, every single day." We need that constant reminder of our true state, apart from God's redeeming work. We should be the best "repenters" in the world! Always first to acknowledge our faults and weaknesses. Quick to apologize.

What if we modeled repentance every day in how we treated each other, as well as those who don't want anything to do with us and our message? I think we'd get much further in our gospel witness if we showed every day what repentance looks like.

As a parent, I've learned that age-old lesson that most things are better caught than taught. The same applies to repentance. Let's practice what we preach.

Of course the challenge is not just in how we behave among those who don't think and act the way we do. The way we treat each other leaves a lot to be desired as well and hampers our witness.

I'm often discouraged by the level of visible and vocal anger, verging on hatred, that characterizes our debate and disagreements, both inside and outside the Christian community. It disturbs me when some within our own camp express their anger with the positions other Christians have taken as the culture has drifted. Certainly there's a range of positions on some hot topics, but I don't see how we can expect to gain any sort of respected cultural voice when we lambaste one another on blogs and other forms of social media.

In the same way that any of us recoil when we see a parent

screaming at a child out of frustration, many have lost whatever respect they may have had as others see us reacting in this way. We all know that when someone resorts to yelling, the battle is over. Let's face it. It's a sign of frustration and defeat. Most followers of Christ don't respond with such vitriol, of course, but it doesn't take many to create an impression. Anger, visible anger, that leads us to say hurtful things is never acceptable Christian behavior whether behind closed doors or in the public square. We need to police ourselves better and stand for civil, loving discourse in the face of whatever may come against us. Loving our enemies. Isn't that what we're called to do? And is a fellow believer ever the enemy? Do some evangelicals consider the LGBT community the enemy? I hope not. Even if, God forbid, they did, doesn't God require us to love them just the same (Matthew 5:44)?

Above All, Hope

Even in the midst of what may seem like a discouraging time—a time of unbridgeable divides within our Christian community and with the community as a whole—there's always hope.

One of my favorite speeches of all time is Abraham Lincoln's second inaugural address. Remember the background? It was Saturday, March 4, 1865. The Civil War had been raging for more than four years. By this point, hundreds of thousands of lives had been lost on the battlefield or to the diseases that ran rampant in the military camps and prisons. Weeks of rain had turned Pennsylvania Avenue into a swampy mire. Yet thousands of people still gathered to hear the president's brief remarks. A little more than a month later, Lincoln would be assassinated. This is what he had to say:

Both read the same Bible and pray to the same God, and each invokes His aid against the other. It may seem strange that any men should dare to ask a just God's assistance in wringing their bread from the sweat of other men's faces, but let us judge not, that we be not judged. The prayers of both could not be answered. That of neither has been answered fully. The Almighty has His own purposes.

Fondly do we hope, fervently do we pray, that this mighty scourge of war may speedily pass away. Yet, if God wills that it continue until all the wealth piled by the bondsman's two hundred fifty years of unrequited toil shall be sunk, and until every drop of blood drawn with the lash shall be paid by another drawn with the sword, as was said three thousand years ago, so still it must be said "the judgments of the Lord are true and righteous altogether."

With malice toward none, with charity for all, with firmness in the right as God gives us to see the right, let us strive on to finish the work we are in, to bind up the nation's wounds, to care for him who shall have borne the battle and for his widow and his orphan, to do all which may achieve and cherish a just and lasting peace among ourselves and with all nations.[5]

Why quote so extensively from this speech, with its ponderous (to our ears), archaic vocabulary? Lincoln had a vision for national unity in the midst of war. He dreamed of a future where reconciliation could unite warring parties. Surely we as followers of Christ can follow his lead, taking a posture of reconciliation in the midst of what often seems like war. Our goal, like Lincoln's, should be peace and hope and love, among ourselves and with those with whom we disagree!

Lincoln had a clear sense of God's providence in the midst of extremely challenging times. There was civil war. Brother against brother. Massive bloodshed. Yet both were claiming God on their side. The president saw a deeper issue at work. He sensed God working through it all to ultimately bring justice. That gave him peace in the midst of the storm—in the midst of his own challenging family situation and his own lifelong bouts of deep depression.

God is still guiding providentially, even as we may feel things sliding out of control. Like Lincoln, we can have the same calm peace and presence of mind that opens many doors.

The context and culture we find ourselves in can be difficult, let's face it. The great news is that the unlikely movement we're part of has survived and thrived in far more challenging times than what we're now facing. The exile in Babylon. The birth of a church with no numbers or resources. Persecution under an evil (Roman) empire. Our playbook today is no different than that of the followers of Christ in those challenging times.

- It starts with unity.

- It's accomplished in the power of the Holy Spirit.

- It's centered on the gospel.

- It's grounded in generosity.

- It's full of love.

- And it's bathed in prayer.

The same Spirit of Jesus that filled and inspired the earliest members of our unlikely movement lives in us today and will lead us to lives of radical generosity and boldness in sharing great news. On we go!

Chapter Three

Finding Common Ground:

Unlikely Relationships

*Tolerance isn't about not having beliefs. It's about how your
beliefs lead you to treat people who disagree with you.*
Timothy Keller, *The Reason for God*

Life is about relationships. Fathers and sons. Mothers and daughters. Husbands and wives. Name a novel, television show, or movie, and I'll show you a story based on relationships—good ones and bad ones. *Breaking Bad*? A husband and father trying his best to support his struggling family and mentor a student. (I'm not saying that he did a great job of it!) *The Walking Dead*? How do I relate to my zombie parents? They've changed!

Relationships are powerful. At their core, they are the foundation of the Christian life. Relationship with God. Relationship with others. It was the goal from the very beginning, back in the Garden of Eden. We were created to relate to God and each other. When Adam and Eve were cast out of the garden, God did not abandon them. He pursued them—a pursuit that culminated at Calvary, in the sacrifice of his son, Jesus. The beauty of God is that he is fiercely relational. Shouldn't we, then, pursue strong loving relationships as well, both inside and outside of the family of believers? It's what the apostle Paul focused on when writing to a group of Christians in the city of Colossae:

———

The beauty of God is that he is
fiercely relational.

———

In this new life, it doesn't matter if you are a Jew or a Gentile, circumcised or uncircumcised, barbaric, uncivilized, slave, or free. Christ is all that matters, and he lives in all of us.

—*Colossians 3:11 NLT*

What a reminder of how it's supposed to be! Christ in all of us who have committed our lives to him, whatever our background. That, in and of itself, is a huge challenge for we who aim to follow Jesus. With the church as divided as it is, one of the hallmarks and beautiful stories that have grown from this journey in Portland has been the amazing way pastors and leaders have built long-term, loving, respectful relationships that have served as the seedbed for every good thing we've seen take place. Whether partnering with public schools, serving kids in the foster care system, or building a new shelter for teenage victims of sex trafficking, it has been a refreshing reminder of the power of true, authentic relationships. Not focused on ourselves, but focused on those in need. Pair that with opportunities to unite in sharing the Good News, whether through festivals, church gatherings, Easter services, or through other evangelistic events, it's a powerful combination!

As a church community, we've been able to work well together and love each other, not because we agree on every detail of church doctrine, but because we've chosen to keep the main thing the main thing.

I like the way my friends Eric Swanson and Sam Williams talk about it. They point back to an idea developed by missiologist and anthropologist Paul Hebert more than thirty years ago in his book *Anthropological Reflections on Missiological Issues*. (Catchy title.) Michael Frost, Alan Hirsch, and Darrell Guder have written about it at great length as well. It's what they call "bounded and centered sets." The concept applies to all our relationships, not just those within the body of Christ.

Bounded-Set Model

In the bounded-set model, we create boundaries, theological borders, and cultural fences to keep clear lines and distinctions between us and those we don't agree with. The main question for individuals who live by this model is, do you believe like I believe? If you and I don't believe the same things, how can we work together? There are certainly times when this model is the appropriate response—when we need to stand firm on what we believe. Of course, the challenge is to know where to stop. Have you heard this one?

I was walking across a bridge one day when I saw a man standing on the edge, about to jump off. I ran over and said, "Stop! Don't do it!"

"Why shouldn't I?" he said.

I said, "Well, there's so much to live for!"

"Like what?" he said.

"Well, are you religious?"

"Yeah," he said. "I'm a Christian."

"Me, too! Are you Catholic or Protestant?"

"Protestant."

"Me, too! Are you Episcopalian or Baptist?"

"Baptist."

"Me, too! Are you Baptist Church of God or Baptist Church of the Lord?"

"Baptist Church of God!"

"Me too!" I said. "Are you Original Baptist Church of God or are you Reformed Baptist Church of God?"

"Reformed Baptist Church of God!"

"Wow! Me, too! Are you Reformed Baptist Church of God, Reformation of 1879, or Reformed Baptist Church of God, Reformation of 1915?"

"Reformed Baptist Church of God, Reformation of 1915!" he said.

I responded, "Die, heretic scum!" and pushed him off.

Bounded-set model. Now you'll never forget it. Sadly, this joke shows the challenges we often face when trying to work together within our own Christian community. Imagine the fences and barriers between communities much further apart, whether those between us and those of other faiths or no faith, or with the LGBT community, where the gulf has become a chasm of misunderstanding.

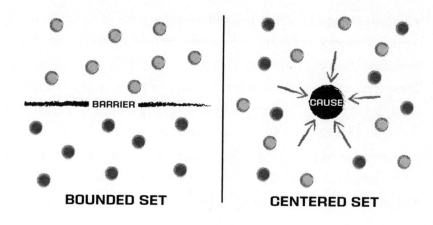

Bounded Sets vs. Centered Sets

Centered-Set Model

In the centered-set model, the question is simply this: Do you care about what I care about? Or, for our purposes: Do you care about what Jesus cares about? It's a powerful question and one that could challenge our thinking on a daily basis. We may have severe disagreements with someone, but when it comes to an issue close to Jesus's heart, can we work together? Is it possible to set aside our differences for a time—for the good of the community—to care about the things Jesus cares about? Does that mean we are compromising? Does it mean we have watered down the gospel? Absolutely not. If our actions together are in line with the heart of God—serving children, protecting the weak, feeding the hungry—doesn't that bring glory and honor to him? Doesn't that open relational doors for the Good News to be shared?

Our Portland experience suggests that great relationships are possible around common-ground issues, even with those with whom we disagree. In fact, I would say these sorts of unlikely relationships should be boldly and eagerly pursued by every one of us who does our best, imperfectly, to follow in the footsteps of Jesus. These relationships can work if we'll focus on the outcomes we long to see come about. Thriving public schools. Kids in foster care who are well cared for and their families supported. The needs of our homeless friends and neighbors addressed. You name it! We can work together and partner on the issues we are all passionate about without pretending to agree on issues of contention.

The Jesus Model

Jesus lived a life of radical inclusiveness, having "table fellowship" with those far outside what would have been socially and religiously acceptable for a rabbi of his day. Having women follow him around and financially support him? Mary Magdalene, a woman known to be loose, spending money on expensive perfume and pouring it on his feet? Enjoying parties with tax collectors and other collaborators with Rome? They were all way out of bounds in his day. And of course he heard about it from the religious establishment.

What about the time he spent hours alone (in a visible, public place) with a heretical woman who turned out to be a serial adulterer? Jesus later told an infuriating story in praise of this same heretical bunch. Most Americans know it as the story of the Good Samaritan. In fact, we have Good Samaritan Laws, protecting people from being sued if they help a stranger in need. In Jesus's time, to even talk to the religious establishment about a "good" Samaritan was an intentional affront, a challenge to their traditional mindsets.

Mirroring the life of Jesus, I believe it is entirely possible to maintain my strong beliefs as a Christian while happily working with people who do not hold all the same beliefs as I do. Even if someone doesn't agree with me about the right to life for an unborn child, that doesn't mean I can't work with them on efforts to combat domestic abuse. It's precisely these common-ground relationships that can build bridges of better understanding to share the gospel.

Centered-set thinking is common-good thinking, common-ground thinking. Tim Keller talks about the church being a "counter-culture for the common good." I love that.

CityServe Portland marked a first for many people within our community—Christians and non-Christians alike. Massive cultural chasms were bridged in the name of the common good, and many lives were touched. But arguably one of the more prominent firsts was the relationship forged between then Portland mayor Sam Adams and several of us in Christian leadership.

How Change Begins

Our relationship with Sam became central to what the churches were able to accomplish as we partnered to meet needs in the city. People often ask me, "How did so much get done in such a radically liberal city?" This question makes me grin. Though I would agree that Portland is well to the left on the sociopolitical spectrum—and Sam would affirm that proudly (while saying he prefers the term "progressive")—I also know that "left" and "right" don't have to stop us when it comes to the kingdom. To me, one of the best, most tangible expressions of my Christian love is directly related to the quality of relationships I cultivate within the community, especially with those with whom I might disagree on some issues.

The relationship Sam and I have is one of mutual respect—one that looks past our differences to the good that we can accomplish together. We've both grown as we've gotten to know one another better.

Like any relationship, ours developed slowly, and by that I mean *trust* developed slowly. Sam has been involved in politics since he was eighteen. When I first met Sam, he'd risen from being former mayor Vera Katz's chief of staff to one of four Portland city commissioners.

The first city official we met with to ask how we could serve was then-mayor Tom Potter. But Portland maintains a unique form of government, with each commissioner holding a significant amount of clout, leading major bureaus. I also wanted to meet with each one of them to talk about CityServe Portland, potential projects, and hoped-for partnerships.

I remember our first meeting with Sam well. Dad and I drove over to his office together. We were both nervous, and so was Sam. In all honesty, Sam was the first prominent gay leader I'd ever met with for a serious discussion. Dad was the first evangelist Sam had ever hosted.

We met in his office at city hall, surrounded by photos and mementos representing his many years in public service. We talked about the needs in the city and our dreams. Dad and I told Sam of wanting to better mobilize churches to love and serve the community. Though he'd never met our team personally, Sam knew exactly who we were. He had a generally favorable impression of my dad due to the previous festival we'd spearheaded seven years earlier at Waterfront Park. Sam's previous boss, Mayor Katz, had been impressed to see 50,000 folks attend a fun, family-friendly outreach weekend right downtown. (Let's face it, politicians "get" crowds.) Sam sensed our intentions were sincere, and seeing the ability of the churches to turn out thousands for a festival left him no reason to doubt something big could happen on the service front as well. Sam even asked if his own church, Trinity Episcopal Cathedral, was involved. It wasn't until later that Sam admitted he wondered if the churches would really deliver, but felt he had nothing to lose since we weren't asking for any city funds.

I am still struck by Sam's openness and lack of defensiveness during that first meeting. Later on, he shared with me some of his past interactions with people he'd perceived to be evangelicals. They had been hurtful—personally and politically. Yet in spite of all that, Sam graciously gave us every opportunity to build a relationship and prove past impressions to be wrong.

This was no small concession on Sam's part. At the time, he thought Westboro Baptist Church was evangelical. It's understandable, I guess. Aren't all Baptist churches evangelical? For a guy who thought our camp included people that would picket military funerals with "God Hates F*gs" and "God Is Your Enemy" signs, to be willing to even talk to us was amazing.

This spoke volumes to me—and still does!

Sam was more concerned with the needs of the city. His general fair-mindedness as a public official, progressive as he was regarding LGBT rights and abortion rights, encouraged Dad and me. So, we cautiously entered into discussions and a working relationship with Sam, as well as many other city officials.

Learning to Love, Not to Leverage

I don't believe in leveraging people to achieve what you want. Using people never works in the long run. It can't last. It was only the fact that Sam and I had found common ground on meeting people's needs that our relationship thrived.

This didn't mean we had to leave our convictions at the door. We never hid our motivation. We believe wholeheartedly in evangelism and are excited to join with believers all around the world to hold evangelistic festivals. It's not as though Sam or anyone in Portland weren't aware that Dad is an evangelist and that the job of an evangelist is to introduce people to Jesus! But we found commonsense ways to work through initial concerns, such as "Is this offer of service really just a way to proselytize?" Absolutely not. The offer of service was just that. Service. Love in action. We understood that there were times and places and ways to introduce Christ effectively, and other ways that broke trust. The fact that we never hid our love for Christ as our motivation helped build that trust. There was no bait and switch. We were authentically ourselves, and so was Sam.

We must always be mindful that our Christian goals don't supersede the love ethic of Christ. He wanted to heal, to mend, to encourage, and ultimately to save, and he accomplished this by loving people wherever they were in life. The apostle John must have remembered seeing his master touching people with healing hands, going to meet folks with eager feet, and speaking to those he aimed to serve with kind words when he penned, ". . . let us not love with words or speech, but with actions and in truth" (1 John 3:18).

The context of this verse is the church. John first encourages the church's members to love one another. It is by those actions that others will see that we are a community worth belonging to. That same love should spill over into our everyday lives as we seek not only to love our brothers and sisters in the church—hard enough on its own sometimes—but to love our neighbors in the same way we love ourselves.

The love of Jesus isn't a love that makes sense to *me,* is convenient for *me,* aligns with *my* sociopolitical views, or a love that empowers *my* own agenda. Can we even call that love? Sometimes the hardest thing for me to do is actively love those in my own church the way I should, with sacrifice (1 John 3:16). But if I don't actively love those closest to me, how will I be able to love those outside my faith community?

———

> The love of Jesus isn't a love that
> makes sense to *me,* is convenient
> for *me,* aligns with *my* sociopolitical
> views, or a love that empowers *my*
> own agenda.

———

It's tough to love. At my core, I am selfish and in desperate need of Christ to help me see and respond to the needs of others. This is what Christ wants. It really has nothing to do with our own wants, or convenience, or agenda. It has everything to do with Christ, what he wants, and what he demands from those who seek to follow him.

It is a love that demands pure motives with our ambition to incite community change.

It is a love that's willing to sacrifice—like the kind Sam showed in entering into a working partnership with us even though Christians had condemned him in the past.

It is a love that enables us to maintain our convictions on clear theological issues and seek to share the Good News.

It is a love that makes no concession to prejudice and does not allow preconceived notions to dictate our efforts to join with those we seek to minister to and with.

Dad and I knew many in Portland hadn't had the chance to really get to know us as a larger group of Christ-followers. Stereotypes abounded, and overcoming those was certainly part of our motivation. What better way to do so than to live as honest and authentic witnesses for Christ as we loved unconditionally. We found that being a witness for Christ is above politics and is megarelational.

It was that first conversation in Sam's office that led to his representing the city in front of six hundred pastors at Cedar Mill Bible Church as we publicly launched CityServe and prepared for CityFest.

It was a drizzly Portland day. I met him in the lobby and escorted him to the front row, where a young band led the packed room of leaders in modern worship songs. It was the first time he'd ever set foot in an evangelical church.

Can you visualize it? Arms in the air in worship. Rock-style music. If you've taken friends to church who haven't been before, you know the feeling. All of a sudden you become hyperaware of every nuance and element. Half of you is trying to worship while the other half is trying to sense how your friend is feeling.

Afterward, Sam said to me, "Kevin, I'm an Episcopalian—raised in it and confirmed at the age of eleven. In all these years I've never heard worship music like that. It was very moving." He loved the quality of it, but even more, he sensed the obvious enthusiasm and joy— and so many hipsters!

Stereotypes were beginning to crumble.

It came time for Sam to speak.

"I just want to acknowledge this incredible sense of passion in this room," said Sam before he read Mayor Potter's proclamation. "You can count on my support for CityServe, and I hope that it's a tradition that will be ongoing and will spread through communities throughout the United States."

Then he read the proclamation, and he got a standing ovation from the packed auditorium! Why was that?

I think the leaders in that room knew we'd had little to no relationship with our city leaders. We were appreciative of Sam's willingness to come onto our turf and graciously offer the city's support for churches that desired to engage more actively in serving. Clearly, it wasn't only Sam's stereotypes that began to crumble. It was ours as well. Pastors began to see the city in a different light. We began to see our city leaders as allies and fellow servants of the common good. They were clearly hardworking leaders doing their best to make a difference in often tough situations.

I talked with Sam after the gathering, and he seemed genuinely moved to have been received so warmly by folks he thought had nothing in common with him, whom he thought might even hate him and his LGBT community. Nothing could have been further from the truth. But Sam didn't know that, and yet he was still willing to step out into the unknown, not really understanding who or what an evangelical was.

It was later in our relationship that Sam told me how, on that night, he began to realize how skewed his views were. He knew that for many Christians, the immediate stereotype for the LGBT community was based on media portrayals of, as Sam puts it, the "scantily clad dancer on the gay pride parade float." And he knew the same was true for himself. He had believed far too many sensationalized media stories that painted all evangelicals in a one-dimensional, negative light. When he joined me in New York City to share the Portland story with one hundred fifty pastors at Tim Keller's Redeemer Presbyterian Church—he's now in the mode of helping me cast this vision of partnership all around the world—he was embarrassed to admit his flawed views. "I considered myself a pretty educated guy. I thought I had an accurate understanding of evangelicals," Sam said, "but I was clueless."

By August 2008, Sam had become mayor-elect. The church community had planned a major Palau festival to share the Gospel and celebrate the work that had been accomplished through CityServe. We asked Sam and Commissioner Nick Fish to join us on stage to help thank those in the crowd who had served in the hundreds of projects throughout the city. Sam was in fine form that day. "This has been the largest, most successful community service effort in the history of Oregon," he shared from the stage. "Now, let's make this an annual activity!"

To be honest, none of us church leaders had really talked about how or whether we'd sustain the effort. An annual activity? We knew it would be a lot of work. But, to Sam's credit, it was what we needed to do. After all, what would it have said to the community at large, and to Sam in particular, if that had been the end of it all, at least in a visible way? And we were seeing such great results!

Trusting Through Challenges

Trust is often built as we go through challenges together. Sam and I experienced that firsthand. Unfortunately, Sam has gotten flak for his involvement in our efforts. In fact, not long after we started working together, Sam asked me, "Do you get any heat because of our friendship and what we do with CityServe?"

I was kind of surprised by the question.

"No," I responded. "None at all, actually."

I still remember the chagrined look on his face.

"Well," he said, "I'm taking heat for my friendship with you."

Our friendship was far more of a risk for Sam than it was for me. I'm more than a little embarrassed not to have thought of what Sam was dealing with from parts of his community. Some felt animosity toward people from a community they felt had abused and disparaged them and stood in the way of their achieving their hopes and dreams. If nothing else, this was a sobering reminder of the work left to be done. The bridges left to be repaired—or completely rebuilt.

The fact is, all good endeavors involve risk. Sam was feeling it. Eventually, we would feel it as well.

It makes me appreciate him that much more. And his response to the critics? It's always the same: "Come talk to me when you can mobilize thousands of people to serve with no strings attached."

As the mayor of everyone in Portland, it made no sense to work with just the folks he agreed with politically or socially. How could he turn down offers of practical help that came with no requests for funding? As he has said many times in his four years as mayor, the only group he could count on to offer quick and effective volunteer help in such great numbers was this growing relational network of Christ-followers. What a testimony. And what a friendship.

But we quickly realized that while he and I may have worked through some of our trust issues, the same couldn't necessarily be said for other leaders around us. That's when Sam and I started hosting gatherings with other pastors and leaders, including larger public meetings as well as some quiet ones. There is one in particular that will always stand out in my mind.

Sam and I had put together a small gathering of leading pastors and prominent LGBT leaders. A little awkward silence is good for the soul, but the first time we met in this way, Sam got caught in traffic. There we were in Sam's conference room in city hall. Six pastors from the largest churches in the area. Six leaders from influential LGBT organizations in the city. It felt like a middle school dance. None of us had met before, and no one said a word. I finally ventured to the other side of the room. (Yes, I'm embarrassed to say we were sitting on opposite sides of a big table.) I stuck out my hand and introduced myself to a well-dressed gentleman. His response was polite, yet curt: "I don't know what the agenda is for this meeting. I'm just here because Sam invited me." Awkward! Sam finally arrived, and what he said was masterful:

> *We're not here to force agreement. This is not a meeting where we from the LGBT side are going to pressure these churches to stand with us on gay marriage. That's not going to happen. But Kevin and I have become good friends and have realized that we have way more in common than we ever thought possible. And the fact is, nothing but good has come from us getting to know one another. We thought it might be good for the community as a whole if we did that here and now.*

Wow! What a way to start a meeting.

We went around the room and began to tell our stories. Rick McKinley from Imago Dei Community started off with an apology. We hadn't gotten together ahead of time as pastors to plan anything out, so I really had no idea what to expect. Rick just began, led by the Spirit, and said, "We love you, and we're so sorry that some people who call themselves Christians have treated you so badly."

And then, we listened.

It was a profoundly moving experience to hear of the struggle and pain most had experienced in their interactions with Christians. Tears were shed, and friendships were born that last to this day.

In fact, that's where I met Barbara McCullough-Jones, the executive director of the Q Center, Portland's LGBTQ community center. As we got to know one another, I found her to be a delightful woman, more than open to sitting down and getting to know me and other Christ-followers better. It was clear she was willing to not let past experiences color her conversations with me. She was a breath of fresh air.

Once we got to know each other, she asked me to come and speak at one of the monthly gatherings at the Q Center. With some fear and trepidation, I accepted.

That rainy Thursday evening turned out to be a delightful hour-long conversation in front of the full room that gathered. Our time together gave me a chance to hear the painful experiences of some of the audience members, and also an opportunity to answer some of Barbara's great questions. One of my favorites: "Kevin, I don't consider myself to be particularly religious, but I am spiritual. One of my favorite songs has always been 'Amazing Grace.' Can you tell us about a time when you experienced this kind of grace?"

Talk about an open door! What an honor to be able to joyfully talk about the gospel in a personal way, and to share why it is Good News for all of us that receive it. I came away from my time at the Q Center encouraged. We all long for unconditional love and grace. I heard it from nearly everyone I spoke with there. And I find nothing more exciting than to be able to share that love and grace—offered to us by Jesus Christ—with anyone I meet. And to trust God with the results.

This friendship with Barbara and Logan Lynn, the PR/community outreach director for the Q Center, was put to the test, so to speak, several months later. The front page of the *Oregonian* announced an "anti-gay" church was coming to a very progressive neighborhood in southeast Portland. As you can imagine, it caused a stir. Some of us would have argued, given the chance, that the church wasn't really antigay in the first place but, instead, was simply trying to be faithful to their understanding of what Scripture teaches. Nevertheless, the media took over and had a field day. I found myself that Saturday morning on my back deck, praying over the phone and counseling with the pastor, a friend who was new to town. Thankfully, Logan had been quoted, saying, "We don't know this church, but we'd welcome them to come visit us so we can get to know them."

My friend Gerry Breshears, a wonderful professor from Western Seminary, was part of the conversation as well. We both agreed: "Take the Q Center up on their offer. Head over there as soon as you can!"

As we had expected and hoped, Logan and Barbara welcomed the conversation. A friendship was built and animosity avoided. The willingness to sit down and talk, despite deep differences, was a blessing all the way around.

About two months after the front-page article, vandals struck the church. They broke windows and painted graffiti—making it clear their anger was a result of the preconceived notions presented in the *Oregonian* article. Homophobic. Bad for the neighborhood.

Guess who was first on the scene, working alongside church members as they cleaned up? That's right. It was folks from the Q Center and the LGBTQ community. Unlikely relationships can sometimes be the most powerful.

Sam: In His Own Words

Sam is a friend. We've learned a lot from each other. Sam listens when I challenge him to take a fresh look at the Bible. To read it for himself and to pray and seek God. He's heard the Good News in a fresh and real way, and that would not have happened without the relationship and the love shown. He knows I disagree with him on many issues, and I love him. And I've learned from Sam the value of taking the time to reach way beyond my comfort zone to build lasting relationships, that it's possible to disagree strongly but still be friends, and that we can actively work on common-ground issues.

Here's a conversation Sam and I had as we reminisced about the beginning of our friendship and that first year or two of CityServe. I wanted to share it, so you could hear the story in his own words.

Kevin: Prior to the CityServe project in Portland, what was your view of evangelical Christians?

Sam: My view of evangelical leaders stems mostly from those whom I have dealt with, interacted with in the past, and my views have changed. I think that is true for those who have worked with CityServe at all levels; their views have changed. Those churchgoers who have been a part of it have told me that their views of the secular world have changed as well.

So the biggest leap of faith that I had to make was to trust that in this partnership we were going to focus on what we agreed to, we were going to act on what we agreed, and that we were going to do that with integrity. There was a clear understanding that this project wasn't a secret recruitment or proselytizing or a project on behalf of building up evangelical churches.

And from the church's point of view—and you'd have to ask them for sure—but I'm sure they had to trust that we (the city) would be giving them meaningful work to do. It's one thing to facilitate a group of churchgoers and parishioners to fix up a building and paint walls and another thing to have them come into the classroom to mentor kids on how to succeed in school.

So the project as a whole required both of us to take risks. Now, one thing that bolstered my confidence early on was your willingness, Kevin (and your team), to talk about some of these issues up front. It also meant a lot that you were willing to have this conversation with the core group of pastors and other church staff we were working with through CityServe.

Kevin: Were you skeptical at all when you first heard of our proposition to organize churches to do this project?

Sam: My former boss had been involved in an earlier festival, and she sent me something about the ability of the Palau organization to bring together churches in the tri-county area and a very strong network that could and did turn out a very large group for these festivals.

So when they approached us with the idea of including a community service component and asking input on that, obviously I was pleased, because we have, like every other city in the world, unmet needs. Some of those needs lend themselves to one-time volunteer efforts.

But I have to say that I came to the proposition after a couple of decades of being involved with this kind of work sort of hopeful that it could be turned into something sustainable—something ongoing in nature, something that would have a longer life than just good deeds associated with the festival.

At the time it was weighing heavily with me that schools and services that were supposed to provide safety-net services for youth were going through a period of deep financial cuts. So this proposition sounded like hope. I never want to be accused of looking a gift horse in the mouth. I was very pleased at the prospect of having hundreds of volunteers as part of the Palau Festival who were willing to do something in Portland. So, yes, I was very enthusiastic about it.

Coming into it, my impression of evangelicals and evangelical churches was not a positive impression overall. But my impression of the Palau Association was that they were not known for stridency on hot-button social issues. So, that was another reason I was relieved.

Kevin: Sam, I mentioned our stories about our respective communities and their reactions to our friendship. But what I didn't share was the scandal. You're very open about that aspect of your political career. Can you share what happened?

Sam: In 2003, a political rival had accused me of having an intimate relationship with a 17-year-old high school graduate who lived and worked in Salem as an intern in the state legislature. I did not break the law, but I lied about the fact that we did have a brief relationship after he became an adult. Eventually, the issue was investigated by the Oregon attorney general, who found "no credible evidence" to pursue legal action. The relationship was legal and consensual, but dumb and a mistake. And lying about it was a huge failure on my part. So, in January of 2005, under media pressure, I decided to tell the truth. It created a media storm.

Kevin: And, as I recall, the news broke just before the second Portland CityServe launch event in February of 2009. You and Commissioner Nick Fish were scheduled to receive a $100,000 check on behalf of the City of Portland from the network of churches represented at the launch. Rick McKinley from Imago Dei Community, Frank Damazio from City Bible Church, and James Martin from Mt. Olivet Baptist Church were the pastors who headed up the joint offering and were onstage to present the check.

Sam: Yes, I was supposed to, once more, say a few words in front of the five hundred church leaders gathered for the CityServe launch at Hinson Baptist Church, and that's where Rick and company were going to present the check. But after the scandal broke, I expected to be cut out of the program. I didn't think CityServe was dependent upon one person, even if that person was the mayor, but I expected to be cut out and disinvited. When that didn't happen, I still expected to be publicly shamed or judged, and that wasn't what happened.

Kevin: I remember gathering our team and several of the church leaders together to discuss if we should ask you, as the new mayor, to send someone else. We had a quick conference call with the key pastors, and it was quickly unanimous: go ahead as planned. Extend love and grace. Not because we were in agreement or felt the incident was okay, but because you had already been scandalized and publicly confessed and we felt that we were called to pray for you and treat you with respect as our mayor.

Sam: I didn't expect that level of understanding and compassion. I got that from your father. I got that from you and from other leaders in the evangelical community. You were all very clear. You didn't like what I'd done, but you were also very clear that we were going to move forward and do good things *together*.

I had made mistakes, but you were supportive, even with my flaws, supportive of continuing to work with me as the mayor moving forward and still believing that the needs were too great and that the opportunity to do good was too profound. It was for me, personally, very moving.

When the scandal hit, I didn't offer to bow out, because what was required of CityServe was for lots of imperfect people to come together around agreement and disagreement and do good work together. So I went into that church very unsure and nervous about what kind of reaction my decision would get. I was pleased that you and the pastors saw the effort as greater than one person, and that the reaction was very humane. Obviously, you were not supportive of what I'd done, and neither was I. My mistakes were very clear. But so was the grace on that day.

The scandal was not only big news in Portland, hitting the front page of the *Oregonian* day after day, but across the country as well, including *Time* magazine. It wasn't just a run-of-the-mill scandal—this was the-first-openly-gay-mayor-of-a-large-city scandal. The minute it hit, Dad and I, along with my brother Andrew, wondered what, if anything, we could do. Dad has always been an amazingly empathetic, loving person who instinctively reaches out whenever he can, offering prayer and biblical counsel. While we guessed this might be the last thing Sam wanted, we texted to say, "Dad would love to meet with you to pray, if you want."

To my great surprise, we got word back almost immediately.

"Yes! Let's meet."

Our mutual friend, Bill Lupfer, then dean of Trinity Cathedral, arranged to have Dad and Sam meet there, on safe, neutral ground. While I wasn't present for the private meeting between the two of them, Dad came out in tears, very moved by the chance to not only deepen his friendship with Sam, but to share, from his perspective as an evangelist, truth and encouragement from Scripture at Sam's greatest point of need.

Dad knew he would never have been able to sit down at that crisis point had Sam not already seen and experienced a very different sort of love and respect than he expected. That was a direct result of relationship, of taking the time to cultivate honest and open friendship.

I appreciate Sam for being my friend even though he knows I can't agree with him on a whole variety of issues, including ones that are core for him. But he's chosen to say, "Let's disagree respectfully, and let's not let that stop us from being friends—from actively working together on the many issues we do agree on."

Relationships are never easy. Especially challenging, unlikely ones, with people whose values or lifestyle or theology may differ from ours. They require work and cultivation. In our frantically busy world, it's easy to neglect them. But there's no substitute for them in our efforts to build the kingdom and see lives and communities transformed. It truly is possible to find and build on common ground with people from very different backgrounds. Jesus modeled it. The gospel requires it. Within our Christian community and without, our impact can be measured by the quality and depth of our relationships. They're not incidental to our mission. They *are* the mission.

Chapter Four

A New Day at Roosevelt High School:

Unlikely Partners

The secret is to gang up on the problem, rather than each other.

—Thomas Stallkamp, former president of Chrysler

I talk a lot about Portland, but I really grew up in the suburb of Beaverton—through the Vista Ridge Tunnel, over the West Hills, and into the valley. That was home. I attended William Walker Elementary School, part of the Beaverton School District. All four of us Palau boys went there through the 1970s. I was student body president in sixth grade and played the lead role of Oliver in the school play. (That was the high-water mark for me socially. It was all downhill from there. Sad!) My youngest brother, Steve, a Wheaton grad, returned to teach there seventeen years ago and has never left. I guess he loved it that much. The students love him, too. (Ever watch *Welcome Back, Kotter?*)

When I was a kid walking those halls, it was 95 percent white (at least it seemed that way to me). I remember one African-American kid, John Johnson, and no Latinos. I would have known. Keith and I spoke fluent Spanish and couldn't find anyone to practice with. Today, the school is majority Latino. It's classified as a high-needs school, with more than 75 percent of the students qualifying for the free and reduced lunch program.

Beaverton as a whole has become a very diverse place, with dozens of languages and people groups represented. It definitely looks different today. But there is no question, Beaverton is still home.

Fast forward forty years from my time at William Walker. There I stood in the back of the largest meeting room at the Beaverton School District headquarters. We were scrambling to add chairs and figure out where to get more coffee, fruit, and croissants. In partnership with Dr. Jeff Rose, the new Beaverton school superintendent, we had decided to try something new. We were so encouraged by our experiences building common-ground relationships with Sam Adams, LGBT leaders, and others that we wondered what might happen if we tried to build similar friendships between Beaverton's fifty-two public school principals and pastors from all over the third-largest town in the state. (I remember Beaverton as a quiet place growing up. Now there are almost 100,000 residents, and it is home to a slew of top businesses, including Nike.) We had planned and prayed for seventy-five people to show up for a simple, relationship-building breakfast. One hundred twenty walked through the doors. Fifty of the fifty-two principals had taken time out of their busy schedules to come, along with more Beaverton pastors than I'd ever seen gathered in one place.

It was an amazing morning. There was a buzz of excitement, mixed with an underlying sense of concern. Was this okay? What about the separation of church and state? Were we breaking any rules by rubbing shoulders and building friendships? Dr. Rose stood up and quieted everyone down.

"We all know there's a line out there," he said. "It's there for a good reason. But in our desire not to cross it, we've stood as far away from it as we can."

I was impressed with his honesty and candor.

"The students and families in our district have many needs," he continued. "Our schools have needs. We're neighbors, the schools and the churches. Rather than staying as far away from the line as we can, I say we get as close to it as possible, shake hands across the line, and work together to improve the lives of our students."

It was a new day for our city and our schools.

That began an amazing journey in good ol' Beaverton. As a direct result of that gathering, as well as the long, hard work of local leaders, more than forty of the fifty-two schools now have a formal church-school partnership. These are churches committed long-term to the prosperity of these schools, offering volunteers, resources, whatever it takes to meet the needs of the students and their families.

From the very beginning of our discussions with pastors and civic leaders around the idea of CityServe, public schools were on the agenda. Sam had come in as mayor with a huge heart for schools. He was trying to improve the educational system throughout the region. No small feat considering the on-time graduation rate across Portland Public Schools hovered just over 52 percent.

For years, various congregations throughout the Portland metro area have served their neighborhood schools, making an impact on the lives of students and staff through mentoring, school cleanup days, and the like. But it had never been tackled in an organized way. No one knew which schools were being served by which churches, what needs were still left unmet, or what schools were still without help.

In many ways, this district-wide gathering was a new step forward—a community linking arms to build trust and meet the greatest needs of the public school system. It was a vision that, in many ways, was birthed out of an unlikely partnership between one church and one school not too far from where we were gathered.

It didn't begin in Beaverton. It began in Portland, as part of that first CityServe effort. It started small, as these things often do. A cry for help from one high school in North Portland. A neglected and nearly forgotten school that had seen, and could still vaguely remember, better days. Roosevelt High School.

The superintendent of Portland Public Schools, Carole Smith, had identified Roosevelt High in North Portland's St. Johns neighborhood as the most challenged urban high school in the city. It was built for 1,600 students in 1922, when the neighborhood was overflowing with young, middle-class families. Yet, by the 1970s, the neighborhood had drastically changed. The once-quiet neighborhood had become one of *the* places for gang activity. The notorious Bloods and Crips gangs from Los Angeles had established outposts in the area. And sadly, a neighborhood that had never experienced gang shootings saw a series of deaths. It may not have been much compared to Los Angeles or Chicago, but it was a shock in much quieter Portland.

Roosevelt High School became synonymous with gang activity. Any parent that could get their child out had done so by 2008. The ones that were left felt stuck. Roosevelt's enrollment had dwindled to four hundred fifty students, and the school was on the shortlist of potential facilities to be shut down. They couldn't field a football team, because the grandstands had been condemned. It was a hard and discouraging place to live. Even harder to receive an education.

Enter Southlake Church, a suburban megachurch twenty miles outside of North Portland in affluent West Linn.

As part of Portland's CityServe efforts, we were working over-time to not only engage churches but the corporate world as well. I personally spent significant time at places like Intel, Wells Fargo, and Nike, meeting with executives to see how CityServe could enhance their existing community service efforts.

In one particular gathering with leaders at the beautiful Nike campus, we were brainstorming about what sort of projects might make sense for them. That's when Mike Bergmann, a manager at Nike, spoke up. "I'm volunteering at Roosevelt High School," he said. "I'm trying to drum up some sort of community support, but it's tough. Come see it."

Wilson Smith, a top designer in Nike's Innovation Kitchen, the legendary design studio that developed the Air Jordan, spoke up as well. "I'm the worship leader at Southlake Church. I think we'd be open to helping."

Within a few days, Mike was leading Wilson and me through the halls of Roosevelt. It was quickly apparent how big the chal-lenge would be. Yet at the same time, deep down, I was excited. I knew something big was in the works.

Wilson took a report back to Southlake's senior pastor, Kip Jacob. He didn't even hesitate. "We've got a couple thousand peo-ple," said Jacob. "We could do something big. We would love to throw ourselves into this as part of CityServe."

Superintendent Smith's response: "Anything you can do for Roosevelt would be wonderful."

Little did I know what would actually be accomplished and

what doors this one unlikely partnership would open for other schools and churches.

In all honesty, looking back, the original idea fit the "drive-by service" model. A church comes into an urban neighborhood with numbers and resources, does the project, and heads back out to the suburbs. I'm not blaming Southlake for that. It was as far as our minds knew to go in those days. The plan was to hold a massive clean-up day, inside and out. Yard work. Landscaping. Painting. It wasn't wrong. In fact, it was extremely helpful—exactly what Roosevelt needed at the time and had asked for.

Kristine Sommers, the outgoing and determined woman who served as Southlake's outreach pastor, jumped on board right away. She began meeting with Roosevelt staff to plan.

You can imagine my shock when I arrived at Roosevelt with my dad and sons on that sunny morning in June. More than 1,000 volunteers were swarming over the campus. They had even rented buses to ferry folks from the church in West Linn.

Kristine's efficiency was on full display everywhere you looked. Keeping that many people meaningfully engaged is a massive undertaking. Everyone had been preassigned to dozens of different teams, from painting to landscaping to cleanup to food prep.

While Southlake members represented the vast majority of the volunteers that day, the word had spread to others, including former Roosevelt Roughriders, current students, and neighboring residents. Mayor Sam Adams was also there along with City Commissioner Amanda Fritz. (It was the first time I had met her, and let me tell you, she totally owned that patch of ground on the southeast corner in front of the school.)

If Southlake's involvement had ended that day, people at Roosevelt would still look back and say they did a lot of good. But a funny thing happened. Without any plan, individuals from South-lake continued showing up afterward. In spite of a twenty-mile commute, members of Southlake got to know the students and began to discover simple ways to serve students and improve the school. The collaborative effort became so dynamic that the principal at the time, Deborah Peterson, asked if Kristine could meet to discuss further opportunities.

"You are here with folks from Southlake almost every day," she said. "Why don't you just office here? You could serve as the on-site volunteer coordinator."

Now, six years later, there are part-time, Southlake-funded staff members with office space at Roosevelt. They run a clothes closet, food pantry, and mentorship program. As it so happens, some key Nike executives also took a vested, long-term interest. They were there for the initial cleanup day but also saw other needs. What about the football field? And the grandstands? What about the track? A few months later, Nike, Anderson Construction, and several other key partners began making plans for a completely renovated sports complex, making Roosevelt's athletic facilities the envy of Portland Public Schools.

Neil Lomax, former NFL quarterback and a member of South-lake, scratched his head after the initial cleanup day, also wondering how God might use him and his gifts to help Roosevelt students. His son, Jack, was a star quarterback at Lake Oswego High School just outside Portland at the time. Neil could have easily continued volunteering to coach his son, but instead felt called to stretch beyond himself and serve the students at Roosevelt, a team that hadn't won a single game in more than five years. Their average margin of defeat was forty-six points per game.

"I just felt an urge," he said. "I didn't know exactly what that meant, but I knew my gift was football. I wanted to know if I could help in some way, shape, or form."

Christian Swain, the new football coach for Roosevelt, was thrilled to have Neil as his volunteer offensive coordinator. It was the beginning of a sometimes wacky, sometimes heartbreaking journey that continues to this day. And the great thing? Roosevelt not only began winning, they made the state playoffs! More important, lives were changed in the process. Individuals like Jerome Smith.

Jerome stood about five feet, six inches. He weighed around 165 pounds. After arriving late to practice several times, Coach Lomax got after Jerome. He was ready to come down hard. Teach him discipline, commitment, and timeliness.

"Coach, it's hard to make it to practice on time on days when I need to get my daughter to daycare," Jerome responded. He needed to borrow a car or take the bus. It got complicated. Football often suffered.

Neil bought Jerome a child car seat, and the friendship deepened. Neil learned more about Jerome's story. He got into his life. And the school found better ways to help.

Jerome wanted nothing more than to be the first in his family to graduate high school. Roosevelt was able to support him through a program called Early Head Start, watching his daughter as Jerome earned his high school diploma. Southlake Church also stepped in, meeting specific needs along the way.

Jerome graduated in 2012. Last I heard, he had an internship at Nike.

Sports are one thing. Academic success is another issue entirely. Roosevelt had among the lowest on-time graduation rates in Portland: only 36 percent. It was one of the reasons why the school had been close to the chopping block for so many years. The on-time graduation rate is one of the key metrics the city and school district have used to measure progress, and Roosevelt simply wasn't making the grade. Yet, with the help of the community, including mentors, volunteers, and support programs, Roosevelt's rate has risen significantly over the past several years. In fact, over the last four years, it recorded a 21 percent gain, reaching a current on-time graduation rate of 53 percent. There is still a long way to go, but there is a sense of hope and vision among the teachers, volunteers, and students. (Between 2010 and 2013, reading scores also went up by 37 percent, math scores increased by 24 percent, and enrollment was up 33 percent, setting the school up for sustained growth.)

Not every effort Southlake has undertaken with Roosevelt has worked equally well. Some programs have flopped. Three years ago Southlake planned to launch a mentorship program with the entire freshman class. The church had plenty of enthusiastic volunteers, but a lack of preparation, communication, and training sunk the big idea. A smaller pilot mentorship program with the football team is beginning this semester. The new mentorship program divides the students into small groups, with about six students per mentor, to take advantage of the church's strongpoint—building relationships. While they hope to expand the program in the future, zeroing in on the football team allows the church to focus on training and matching the mentors carefully.

Southlake and Roosevelt's legacy continues to this day in many ways. The documentary *UnDivided* brilliantly tells the whole story of this unlikely partnership and the incredible turnaround of the school (www.undividedthemovie.com). The film continues to inspire hundreds of churches to consider similar partnerships in their own communities. As the film demonstrates, Southlake has offered so much more than resources and new facilities to Roosevelt. They've built relationships with students and faculty; they've demonstrated unconditional love through continuous involvement. Because of Southlake's willingness to walk through some of life's messiness alongside their neighbors, the gospel is on display in a big way in Portland.

Things aren't simple and easy. Issues still remain. "Southlake isn't saving Roosevelt," said one teacher. "Roosevelt has to save itself. And Roosevelt is saving itself. But it's getting help from lots of outside partners. Southlake is a key, integral player in that help."

Gas on the Flame

Following the initial success at Roosevelt, more and more churches began finding their own Roosevelt—their own ways to serve neighborhood schools. Portland Public Schools also began actively reaching out, holding gatherings and barbecues for volunteers as a way to thank them for their service.

It was at one of these gatherings that Carole Smith, the district's superintendent, and one of her board members pulled me aside.

"The gains at Roosevelt have been way beyond our expectations," Smith said. "Would you be willing to try and find us a church partner like that for every school in the district?"

It was an easy answer. And an exciting one, in fact. Not just for me, but for the dozens of pastors and thousands of individuals who had invested so much in the effort. And now, that same question has been asked by sixteen different districts across the metro area! It was the birth of what we now call the School Partnership Network

(SPN), an initiative dedicated to finding a church partner for every public school in the metro area. And as of 2014, there are more than 252 formal church-school partnerships.

Imagine the impact such partnerships can have on a community! So often we look to the government to fix the schools, to make them better and safer. But what if the church said, "Let us help!"? What if we joined hands with the schools closest to us? The Roosevelt-Southlake story is not just a fluke. Their collaborative success is a direct by-product of good old-fashioned effort—cleaning things up, showing up over and over again, mentoring students, giving of their excess, and establishing their presence in the community. And we're not just talking about service. Southlake is still absolutely committed to sharing the Good News. They still desire to see those kids—and their families—find hope and peace and joy and love through Jesus Christ. It's nothing they are going to push inappropriately during school hours, but it's also not something they are going to hide. They are committed to honoring the boundaries set by the public schools. And they should. They are also committed to remaining a steady presence in the community. In fact, just recently they launched Southlake North, a satellite campus for their congregation. It's right in the heart of the St. Johns neighborhood. More than one hundred neighbors now call it home, including the current principal, Charlene Williams, and her family.

Ripple Effects

The ripples from Roosevelt High School have gone across the country. Detroit, Michigan, is a perfect example.

Few cities have been hit harder by the economic recession than

Detroit. In the past twenty years, the population within the city limits has dropped from 2 million people to 700,000. In some parts of the city, there are blocks of burned-out homes with few residents. The situation is making it incredibly difficult for the city to provide services, including education. Yet the body of Christ is alive and well in the Detroit area, and they are constantly looking for ways to propel the Good News forward, seeking the peace and prosperity of the city.

One of those committed followers of Christ is Bob Shirock. He's the senior pastor of Oak Pointe Church in the suburb of Novi. When I read about what he was doing to unite churches in Detroit, I reached out to him on Facebook. With no awareness of the ongoing Portland story, Shirock and others had begun doing similar things to unite the churches to love, pray for, serve, and share the Good News in the community.

Hearing the Roosevelt story, as well as the other things we had been learning, threw gas on his fire. Before I knew it, Detroit leaders, including Chris Lambert from a great nonprofit called Life Remodeled, were coordinating a meeting with the superintendent of Detroit schools to ask how the churches could serve. Much as in Portland, one specific, high-needs school was identified: Cody High School. It was the toughest school in urban Detroit. Shirock and Chris Lambert upped the ante.

Lambert said the idea for Life Remodeled began with the popular TV show *Extreme Makeover: Home Edition*. He was intrigued by the show but also heard many participants wound up losing their homes due to high taxes or ridiculous utility bills. He wanted to find a way to do a similar give-back but include a support system to ensure the changes last. That's when Lambert and Shirock put their heads together. Shirock had the neighborhood in mind and the volunteer base to move things forward. Lambert had the organization, know-how, and connections. They collaborated with a slew of local organizations, including Detroit Public Schools, the City of Detroit, Governor Rick Snyder, United Way, neighborhood churches, and community groups.

Then, during one week in August 2014, more than 10,000 (that's not a typo) volunteers converged on that one school and the surrounding neighborhood. They provided a new roof and rebuilt the school's entryway, science classrooms, and football field. They also remodeled dozens of neighborhood homes and helped demolish dozens more beyond salvaging, helping create a safer neighborhood. It was a $5 million project that included thousands of General Motors and Quicken Loans employees, in addition to the folks from Oak Pointe, Life Remodeled, and several other key suburban churches, along with a dozen neighborhood churches.

As with Roosevelt in Portland, the vision went way beyond the initial makeover. The plan now is for this to become a multiyear partnership, focusing on mentoring students, supporting staff, encouraging the administration, and serving families. Imagine this sort of effort taking place in cities across the United States. It's happening! The more I talk with city leaders, the more I hear stories just like this. And the great thing? It can expand exponentially as the church continues to *be* the church, together, in our cities.

And the invisible line we all seemed to be so afraid of? It's still there. No doubt. But it doesn't keep us from caring for our kids, serving our neighbors, and building relationships with those who may not be like us in our lifestyles or philosophies yet, at the same time, are exactly like us in need.

It's amazing how fast an initiative like this can grow wings. A few gatherings with local leaders. A few church-school partnerships underway. Before we knew it, the *New York Times* was knocking on our door. It seems the religion writer Sam Freedman had heard about what was going on in Portland. Our mutual friend, Jim Daly, president of Focus on the Family, was the one who tipped him off. (By the way, Focus is another great organization working hard to find creative and effective ways to stay rooted in Scripture and reach out in fresh ways to love, serve, and share the gospel. My hat's off to Jim and the crew at Focus.)

The *New York Times* story captured the journey well. An apprehensive school principal. A leery administrative staff. Tons of questions about why we were serving, what our agenda was, and what our end goal might be. Yet, after years upon years of constant, faithful service, the critics had been quieted. The arguments were nonexistent. And the end result was a win for everyone involved—students being served, a city finding footing, and a community finding, well, community.

"There's no way a school can provide everything a child needs," Charlene Williams said in the article. "So, to know you have a partner, and to have the kids know . . ."

There is power in faithful service.

There is power in faithful service.

No surprise, word has gotten out. Even before the *New York Times* story, I was fielding calls from leaders in more than fifty other U.S. cities, including New York City. With NY CityServe now underway, hundreds of NYC churches of all denominations and ethnicities, across all five boroughs, are working to build bridges, establish new partnerships, and serve the city in a unified way. In fact, my friend Jeremy Del Rio from 20/20 Vision for Schools, plus other great ministries like Young Life, are heading up a long-term effort just like what has happened in Portland and Detroit. The next iteration. Hundreds of public schools served by local churches.

What We Learned with Roosevelt

Even though the Roosevelt-Southlake partnership did thrive and continues to, we definitely learned a few things along the way. When we began, we rushed ahead with just Southlake. Carole Smith said Roosevelt had great needs, and Southlake was ready and willing to step up in a big way. They showed they had both the willingness and the resources to help with a makeover. I'll be forever amazed at how Kip and his crew jumped in so quickly and effectively. But—I'm embarrassed to say—the thought never crossed our minds to gather with the other local churches in the St. Johns area, the immediate neighborhood of Roosevelt High School.

Those churches happened to be smaller and less resourced financially than Southlake. Did they not count? Did they not warrant a gathering so that all the churches could dream and pray together about what could be done to bless their neighborhood high school?

Southlake did an amazing job serving, but it wasn't until I began hearing the rumblings of concern from the churches embedded right in that neighborhood that I realized we'd missed a tremendous opportunity to further strengthen solidarity among Portland churches. When we realized what we'd unwittingly done, I was mortified. Thankfully, those local churches were full of grace-filled people, and the story has a great ending.

We immediately apologized and asked what we could do to build some bridges. The initial tension led to a small gathering of leaders eventually called AllOne Community. It still meets every month, giving local pastors a chance to pray for each other. It also allows them the opportunity to open lines of communication to discover new ways to serve their community together. The gatherings, of course, led to more churches getting involved. Several of them took on the challenge of serving the surrounding elementary schools that feed into Roosevelt. They shared the burden and further connected students to individuals in the neighborhood. Everybody wins with this sort of collaboration.

We've also learned to be careful with our language. We used to call these sorts of initiatives "school adoption." Good intentions, bad application. The word "adoption" conveys a paternalistic mindset. It communicates the idea that the church community is the parent rather than the humble servant we are called to be. Certainly school officials know infinitely more about what they need to educate and serve our children. They also know how volunteers might best help. We can't ever assume we know best. We almost always don't. Maybe for our own children or family, but seldom for an entire school or neighborhood.

Let's face it. In the minds of some, Christians have abandoned the public school system. We homeschool our kids in higher numbers than any other community. We've formed thousands of Christian schools around the nation. Those who feel called to educate their kids in these ways have good reasons to do so, but that shouldn't stop us from working together to bless our public schools.

I've become convinced that our public schools are among the best places to love, serve, and make a difference. Every need that exists in the overall community exists in our schools: hunger, homelessness, family struggles, trafficking, abuse. It's all there. And what better time to deal with these major issues than before they take hold, build habits and lifestyles, and run our society deeper into trouble. Rather than waiting for addiction, violence, or family struggles to take over the life of a twenty-something, what if someone began helping and mentoring them in first grade?

Think of this: Every neighborhood in our country has a school. It's a ready-made place to love and serve. Imagine if every single public school in our country had at least one church that raised its hand (so to speak) and said, "That one is ours." Not in the possessive or controlling sense, but rather in the humble role of a servant. The unlikely partnership between Southlake and Roosevelt is a shining example of what could be for every school.

In Portland, we have a dream that eventually every public school in the Portland-Vancouver area would have at least one church partner.

Now imagine this happening all across the country? There are approximately 100,000 public schools across this great land of ours. There are more than 200,000 churches. Math has never been my strong suit, but even I can see that we have a great opportunity in front of us.

If you're not already, I challenge you to prayerfully consider doing something to serve your neighborhood school. This kind of leadership within our communities not only strengthens the lives of young people, it also touches the lives of the adults working in the education sector. And it clearly impacts families—those closely connected to the children you are serving. Unlikely partnerships can be a little scary at times. They come with some risks. But the positive outcomes, for our schools, our neighborhoods, and for the gospel, are well worth it!

Chapter Five

The Powerful Role of Unity:

An Unlikely Prerequisite

May the God who gives endurance and encouragement give you the same attitude of mind toward each other that Christ Jesus had, so that with one mind and one voice you may glorify the God and Father of Our Lord Jesus Christ.

—Romans 15:5–6

By now you've undoubtedly picked up on the fact that I'm crazy about unity among those who call themselves followers of Jesus. It's one of the things I love most about the work my dad and brother Andrew have done over the years. It's what drew me to the crusade approach right out of Wheaton College. The pleasure of seeing thousands of believers from all sorts of backgrounds worshiping, serving, and sharing the Good News together. It's what has given me so much joy in this Portland journey. It's been a prerequisite for the kind of unlikely outcomes we've seen take place. Should it really matter that much? If every church is doing its own thing well, finding good ways to serve, and is sharing the Good News in their own way, who cares whether we're visibly seen as doing it together? Does unity really matter?

The sad reality is that we are far from being "all one in Christ"— from fulfilling the prayer Jesus prayed in John 17. Most who follow Christ would believe, in theory, that we are all part of the body of Christ, each with our own unique role to play. Sadly, we seldom live up to what we claim to believe about each other.

Too often, through our lack of unity, our lives have told a sad, discordant story. I believe we often sell the Good News short by the way we treat fellow believers, and it mars our witness.

**We often sell the Good News short
by the way we treat fellow believers.**

I can understand the struggle and reticence some feel about working hand-in-hand with those outside the church. It's a delicate balance, but one many of us in Portland have been happy to pursue for the sake of the gospel. Yet inside the church—among brothers and sisters? You'd think our love for each other and our core unity would shine through. Way too often, that's not the case.

Church history bears out the harsh reality of our disunity. Christians fighting one another over doctrine, sometimes to the death! Catholics vs. Protestants. Protestants vs. Evangelicals. It seems like a never-ending cycle. It has led to the creation of tens of thousands of denominations around the world. We who might call ourselves evangelicals seem to fight over anything and everything. It's ironic that our modern evangelical movement in the United States emerged out of the desire of an earlier generation of Christ-followers to find a measure of unity around the gospel.

One hundred years ago tensions were running high in many mainline Protestant denominations as the impact of higher criticism of the Scriptures and Darwin's *Origin of Species* reached high tide.

Concerned, theologically conservative Christians banded together and developed *The Fundamentals: A Testimony to the Truth*, among many other responses. This series of pamphlets focused on defining the fundamentals of the Christian faith and remains a fascinating collection of apologetic writings. Some of these early fundamentalists—remember, at that time it wasn't yet a negative term—wanted to concentrate on fighting the "liberal/modernist" Christians and separating from the changing culture. Others felt led to focus their energies on outreach and evangelism and worried that the fighting would do more harm than good.

In this time of theological crisis, younger leaders like evangelist Billy Graham and R. A. Torrey emerged. They wanted to establish a united front among churches, a way to come together around the central message of Jesus Christ. They kept the gospel vibrant and relevant. Dubbed the neoevangelicals, they were conservative in theological terms but sought innovative ways to put the message of Christ forward in positive, bridge-building ways. They didn't agree with more liberal or progressive views of interpreting Scripture but sought more subtle ways to maintain their conservative views.

Some fundamentalist leaders attacked Billy as a compromiser for not clearly attacking those he disagreed with. They called him a heretic and told their followers to stay away from his citywide crusades. But he led a quiet revolution and helped birth many of the significant para-church organizations and institutions that are still making a difference today. Organizations like Campus Crusade for Christ (now called Cru), *Christianity Today*, Youth for Christ, and Gordon-Conwell Theological Seminary are just a few of the organizations Billy had a hand in starting or encouraging. These agencies were part of a fresh wave of gospel-sharing around the world, and Billy himself brought hundreds of churches together in city after city to share what C. S. Lewis called "mere Christianity." It was this expression that was eventually able to gather Catholics, mainline Protestants, and evangelicals together in visible unity around the Good News.

Billy and his staff worked hard to create a platform and model under which hundreds of individual churches could maintain their individuality and lesser theological distinctions while joining together in unity. As denominations proliferated in the United States, there was a felt need to have times and seasons to come together, and the Billy Graham Crusade became the gold standard of Christian solidarity.

It's interesting to note that in no other time in history have so many denominations lived side by side than in America today. However, what used to be a powerful mosaic of denominational unity now looks like broken glass lying on the floor—shattered fragments that lack cohesion and a shared vision.

In light of our historical divisions and current fragmented existence, let's consider the words of Jesus as he prayed for his called-out ones, the church.

> *I'm praying not only for them [his earliest disciples]*
> *But also for those who will believe in me*
> *Because of them and their witness about me. [That's us!]*
> *The goal is for all of them to become one heart and mind—*
> *Just as you, Father, are in me and I in you,*

So they might be one heart and mind with us.
Then the world might believe that you, in fact, sent me.
The same glory you gave me, I gave them,
So they'll be as unified and together as we are—
I in them and you in me.
Then they'll be mature in this oneness,
And give the godless world evidence
That you've sent me and loved them
In the same way you've loved me.

—John 17:20–23, The Message

Jesus emphasized the importance of Christian solidarity, because he knew that it would be one of the main ways the world would *see* him: through us and our unity. The evidence of God's love to the world is to be found in the church, by our sharing the Good News and through our love for each other and for the community as a whole. Jesus prayed that we would stand unified as visible, tangible evidence of his love. We are to be one just as he and God the Father are one. What a tremendous opportunity!

When we quibble over small doctrinal issues, when we publicly ridicule our own leaders for their mistakes, we greatly diminish the beauty of the gospel and our story. Imagine what might have happened to our opportunities to serve in Portland had we reacted to Sam's scandal the way some evangelicals react to one another via online articles, blogs, and Twitter.

Some suggest that the Internet offers a new level of Christian accountability—that we are supposed to hold our leaders publicly accountable. But I wonder how much of that is just an excuse to blast leaders we don't agree with. It's shameful to air our dirty laundry in public, not following principles clearly laid out in Scripture.

When you read the Proverbs, King Solomon emphasizes how wisdom and discernment are found in restraint—the restraint of our mouths. If we are quick to attack one another, is this evidencing wisdom? Has the church exchanged its fear of God for a license to travel the pathways of the foolish?

Jesus prayed for our maturity in unity. It doesn't mean we must agree with one another on everything. When we operate under that canopy of love and grace, then unity becomes a strength we use to do good for others and to share the love of God's gospel. Isn't that the ultimate goal for all Christians?

I've already talked about the first meetings I had with Sam Adams. One thing I've not shared yet was how he viewed the unity among churches. He absolutely assumed it! He had higher expectations for it than I did, and I've made it much of my life's work to try to bring churches together for the common good to share the Good News and work.

When I first described the vision of CityServe to Sam (and I've found this to be true among many others who aren't actively involved in their local congregations), he assumed all the churches were eager and willing to work together! Wouldn't it be great if it were that easy? I had to explain to Sam and others the complexities of working for Christian solidarity. As I'll often say, "It's taken the church two thousand years to splinter into thousands of distinct denominations and streams. Please be patient while we try to get some of us to work together!"

How Do We Build Unity?

How do we work for unity within the body of Christ? In many ways it's simple. It's about relationships and the sort of centered-set thinking we talked about in Chapter 3. In Portland, we've invested heavily in creating the space for relationships of trust to be built among pastors and leaders.

These types of relationships take time but are so worthwhile. And we're seeing the results. A business leader in the Portland area with a passion for building the kingdom has a 40,000-acre ranch out in a remote part of eastern Oregon. That ranch has become a relational haven for those of us who have made the trek there to build friendships focused on seeking the peace and prosperity of Portland. Taking thirty-six hours together to fish, ride ATVs, and shoot guns, with no agenda other than getting to know one another and pray, has built a strong foundation. If you were to see us as a group, you would probably laugh. So many different backgrounds. So many different walks of life. Urban hipsters. Suburbanites. Pastors. Business leaders. All of us together in mission—to share the Good News and bless our city. We camp and talk and dream and pray together under the stars and around a campfire, sharing our struggles and our fears. And together, we kick around the question: What might Portland look like in twenty years if we could actually stick together that long and work to further the Good News in both word and deed?

Obstacles

Someone once asked me, "What keeps churches from wanting to work together?" For some, it's a genuine desire to avoid confusion and perceived compromise. They feel that it's intellectually and spiritually dishonest to pretend to agree when there are disparities on points of doctrine. The challenge, of course, is that we've all seen where this leads.

Take, for example, the denomination that became known as the Plymouth Brethren. Dad and his family came to a living faith in Jesus Christ in the town of Ingeniero Maschwitz, a suburb of Buenos Aires, Argentina. Mr. Rogers (not the sweater-wearing Presbyterian minister singing about a beautiful day in the neighborhood) was an executive with what would now be called Shell Oil Company. He was a very committed member of the Plymouth Brethren from the United Kingdom. He had moved to Argentina for work but viewed all of life as an opportunity for ministry. In his free time, he would go door to door, handing out copies of the Gospel of John (with Psalms and Proverbs) and inviting people to join him for a Bible study. It was my dad's mother who first came to Christ through Mr. Rogers. Later his father. Then many other family members.

The Plymouth Brethren were never numerically strong but wielded an influence far beyond their numbers. They influenced leaders such as D. L. Moody and R. A. Torrey. They were biblical literalists, trying to recapture a radical New Testament Christianity. This meant, in practical terms, that women couldn't speak in services, there were no musical instruments used in worship, and there were no paid clergy. The congregations were entirely elder led. There were many great aspects of this attempt to live as the early church did, and Dad experienced this as he grew up among the Brethren. Young people were taught wonderfully and knew the Word to a degree that would seem astonishing today. Dad was teaching younger kids and preaching by the time he was fifteen. I've always held the Plymouth Brethren in high regard, for their passion, their perseverance, and their commitment to Scripture.

But, in those early years in Argentina, Dad also experienced negative aspects. The Brethren split to a remarkable degree over very fine points of doctrine. Members in some of these assemblies (as they're called) could not receive communion even from other Brethren assemblies without proper vetting. This meant you had to acquire letters from the elders of your home assembly to present to the elders of the local assembly. If you weren't the right sort of Plymouth Brethren—and remember, this is in Argentina, and the Brethren were just one tiny part of the very small evangelical movement in the nation—then you weren't welcome to join in worship or take communion. As my Dad used to say, "The Brethren could give an amazing exposition on John 17 and the beauty of Christian unity. They just didn't practice it to any noticeable degree!"

I know that's not the case in many Brethren assemblies today. We have collaborated with many who are open and loving and excited to work with others in unity. It just wasn't Dad's experience growing up in Argentina in the 1940s.

What keeps us from greater unity today? There are many reasons, but one is pride, pure and simple. Sometimes larger, thriving churches feel they've got it all covered. When your church is full to overflowing, it's hard to believe you need others. Thankfully, there are myriad examples of large, thriving churches that truly care about their peers in town. They're willing to take the time to get to know other pastors. They believe what the Bible teaches about our being one body with many different parts, each with an important function.

In the United States, with our desire to be professional and effective, to be focused on growth, it's hard for some to justify the "time wasting" that's involved with building relationships with other churches in town. To them, it's a distraction from the mission and vision statements they've crafted, sometimes with the help of paid consultants.

There's nothing wrong with working on becoming better managers of our time, but sometimes we're more influenced or distracted by resources on leadership development and management than on Scripture and the leading of the Holy Spirit. I've seen the very churches that should be leading their cities be the ones least likely to care about broader, unified efforts to impact the community. When we talk about unity, we're not talking primarily about working on a series of big events or programs. Rather, we're talking about an attitude of the heart. It's caring about the success of others and consciously choosing to see the contribution of our local congregation or nonprofit as one part of a greater whole. That may seem nebulous, but over time it's the foundation for any sort of collective impact.

In my experience, one great way to observe the humility and godliness of pastors is to listen to how they talk about and treat fellow pastors.

Do they pray for others?

Rejoice in the success of others?

Do they carve out valuable time to encourage their fellow workers?

I am so blessed to see the vast majority of the churches in Portland loving and serving one another. This includes almost all of the large "busy" churches. To me it's the single greatest evidence of the presence of the Spirit of Jesus Christ living and expressing himself through us. We rejoice in each other's victories, we pray together, we take occasional retreats together, we share the Good News together, and we challenge each other. We've built on the great foundation the earlier generations of pastors built when they went away for 3-day prayer summits.

Two years ago, some pastors in the area shared a desire to encourage each other as they prepared for Easter. They wanted to gather together, pray for one another, and hold each other accountable in their efforts to clearly proclaim the gospel message during their Easter services. Their request? To hear from Dad and be inspired by his fifty years of experience in sharing the Good News around the world and to ask him questions. Dad and I were more than happy to help coordinate the effort. Fifty churches covenanted to pray for each other during Easter. One thousand people gathered to pray the Wednesday before Easter. And just in those churches, more than 1,600 people publicly committed their lives to Christ. Not only that, but more than six hundred fifty were baptized.

The fact that Portland pastors love and encourage each other is what keeps us going year after year. There's an almost unspeakable joy to feel you have true brothers and sisters in the journey. People who love you and have your back. Who will call you out when needed, who will hold you accountable for the work you've been given, and who will pray for you on a regular basis.

One key group that has developed over the past dozen years in Portland is called BIC (Brothers in Christ). It was founded by Don Krahmer, a prominent partner in a large downtown law firm with an unbelievable capacity to network. I love meeting folks and connecting people, but I've never met someone like Don. He's relentless in his desire to build a band of brothers, key business leaders from across the denominational spectrum. His simple vision—to meet regularly to love and support each other in our shared faith in Christ. Every month, at the Arlington Club in downtown Portland, seventy-five business leaders meet for breakfast and to hear about one man's spiritual journey. We also have an annual retreat at the Oregon Coast.

Several things set BIC apart, including Don's insistence on

getting Catholics, mainline Protestants, and evangelicals together. (There's now a SIS—Sisters in Spirit—that meets on a regular basis as well.)

This group has been such an encouragement to me, as well as many others. It's so exciting to find new brothers across the metro area and to see the common ground we share. We don't agree on everything. And that's okay. We can encourage one another in Scripture and draw each other closer to Christ.

One of the things that always set Dad apart, back in the day, was the way he lifted up Christ and shared the Good News in Latin America without getting into the often hot debate between evangelicals and Catholics. He simply lifted up Christ—his love, his beauty, the meaning of his sacrifice, and the opportunity to know for sure that you have a relationship with him and are secure. Dad never attacked or got into petty arguments. And for that, he was respected.

That hasn't meant that misunderstandings haven't arisen, even recently.

As part of a series of festivals and outreaches we have held in Argentina over the years, Dad had the chance to become friends with the archbishop of Buenos Aires, Cardinal Jorge Mario Bergoglio.

The first time they met privately, Dad was struck by Cardinal Bergoglio's quiet humility. No pomp or show, just a quiet time of reading the Bible and praying together. When it was time to go, Jorge asked Dad, "Would you lay hands on me and pray for me?"

You know Cardinal Bergoglio as Pope Francis, and he's continued to model a fresh approach to the papacy, emphasizing solidarity with the poor and a remarkable openness to brothers and sisters in Christ from outside the Catholic Church.

When Jorge was announced as the new pope, Dad was excited. Who wouldn't be excited for their friend to receive such an honor from their peers? Dad posted a video in Spanish on Facebook to his more than 500,000 Latino followers to simply congratulate his friend and tell him he was praying for him. Let's just say the response was a reminder that we have a long way to go in learning how to express ourselves with love and grace within the body of Christ. Hundreds upon hundreds of angry posts followed. *Luis Palau is a heretic. He's abandoned the gospel.* On and on it went.

Had Dad changed his theology? Become a Catholic? No. All he'd done was acknowledge his friendship with Pope Francis.

Of course there are differences between denominations. If that weren't the case the thousands of denominations wouldn't exist. But at the heart, there is still a common core of historic Christian belief among most denominations that can be built upon and emphasized, exemplified in the early Nicene Creed from the fourth century:

1. We believe in one God, the Father Almighty, Maker of heaven and earth:

2. And in Jesus Christ, his only begotten Son, our Lord:

3. Who was conceived by the Holy Ghost, born of the Virgin Mary:

4. Suffered under Pontius Pilate; was crucified, died and was buried: He descended into hell:

5. The third day he rose again from the dead:

6. He ascended into heaven, and sits at the right hand of God the Father Almighty:

7. From thence he shall come to judge the quick and the
    dead:

8. I believe in the Holy Ghost:

9. I believe in the holy catholic (universal) church: the
    communion of saints:

10. The forgiveness of sins:

11. The resurrection of the body:

12. And the life everlasting. Amen.[1]

It's a joy to see and celebrate historic unity in the midst of the
great diversity of the body of Christ and this amazing movement of
which we're all a part.

I know it seems much easier and more effective to do things
alone. Here in the United States, we value effectiveness more than
anything else. We're the pragmatists of the Christian faith: get
things working well, efficiently, so we can see immediate results.
If it works, then no other justification is needed. We tend to value
numbers and financial security as the prime proofs of fruitfulness
and blessing.

These by-products of ministry are not bad in and of themselves,
of course. We long to see thousands of people come to our festivals
and outreach efforts around the world. We desire to see more and
more churches growing, with new folks coming to faith in Christ.
And it is good to celebrate the work God accomplishes through us.
The sad reality is, however, that those fruits of our labor can also
lead to carnality of the worst sort—a comparison-based life of feeling superior and judging other churches or ministries as weaker and

less effective when in reality it may simply be a matter of location. Some are serving in tougher neighborhoods, cities, or nations, or they have fewer resources with which to operate.

Unity doesn't mean uniformity. It doesn't mean pretending we all do life the same way or agree on everything. We will *never* all agree—there are too many topics, too many problems, too many solutions, too many perspectives. Unity is more of an attitude of love and humility, recognizing that there is no way my limited experience can be the whole story. If the goal is to reach and help incite change in a city, then there's so much more needed than my very narrow experience.

———

Unity is more of an attitude of love
and humility, recognizing that there is
no way my limited experience can be
the whole story.

———

Unity among brothers and sisters in Christ is part of the beauty of the gospel. I love to see large churches modeling humble solidarity with others. Southlake Church is well resourced with people and finances. They didn't *need* a project like Roosevelt High School and could have happily continued investing in their own programs to meet the spiritual needs of their own people. But Southlake humbled themselves, joined with the collective CityServe efforts, and asked how they could best be used. That's power. And the community is the better for it. It's cost them far more than money and time. They've lost members who couldn't see how investing so much in a community twenty miles away made sense. That will always make me sad, but the church's willingness to continue shows others that God's love is not a drive-by kind of love. Rather, it's a love that stays. It's a love that digs in and searches for solutions when problems seem too large.

Seeing Past Ourselves

Bringing churches together demands humility from everyone involved. We have to genuinely love every church and believe they're a beautiful part of the body of Christ. We must believe that in God's providence they exist in their neighborhood "for such a time as this" to reflect the beauty of Christ. Big churches, small churches, thriving ones, struggling ones, black, Latino, Slavic, young, old, hipster, white church planters, and traditional Pentecostals, all reflect a unique facet of the body and all contribute to reaching people. My prayer is that we actually believe that we need each other. I know that can be very hard. It requires renouncing parts of our American mindset, which values self-reliance above almost all else.

We need to elevate and celebrate humility within leadership. I find that the more curious I am about what God is doing in other churches, the more open doors I find. Folks can tell when you care or when it's fake or simply a means to an end. The more I care about other churches and their success, the more common ground can be found around the much bigger picture: the fact that we need each other to have any hope for the gospel to truly move in our cities.

If we desire to serve the Lord in our communities, then we need to focus on three things.

First, we need to believe what the Bible teaches: that we are one body. We desperately need each other. It's a lie that we can exist and thrive in isolation.

Second, we need to experience the joy of knowing other churches. We should practice speaking well of them. Stop yourself from repeating gossip and passing along emails and links attacking fellow believers. It's carnality of the worst sort to rejoice when a pastor falls, to pile on when someone has messed up, to talk poorly about other churches when they struggle. Tell the success stories of others, not to take credit, but to make it clear that you believe their success is your success.

Finally, we need to find at least one project in our towns or neighborhoods that we can do together with those other churches. Go see the right leaders, and ask, "How can we serve you?"

Unity in Action

Advent Conspiracy is a great example of this unity we seek. Started in 2006 by Rick McKinley (pastor of Imago Dei Community), Greg Holder (pastor of The Crossing in St. Louis, Missouri), and Chris Seay (pastor of Ecclesia Church in Houston, Texas), this powerful project is finding ways to help people think differently about Christmas, a tradition in which many of us, regardless of our faith perspective, take part.

I'm not sure if you could find a bigger fan of Christmas than I am. I have so many spoken and unspoken traditions that have to be followed. Where we put the tree. When we put up the lights. What music we listen to and when. The myriad of films that must be watched as we build up to the holy grail of Christmas movies: *It's a Wonderful Life*. It drives my normally patient family crazy.

At the same time—if I'm honest—the frantic nature of it all can also lead to feelings of stress. Expectations, met or unmet, can lead to discouragement. A lack of fulfillment. A feeling of selfishness. And I know I'm not alone. Many feel that way about Christmas and the gradual shift toward consumerism.

That's what led McKinley, Holder, and Seay to start Advent Conspiracy.

"We all want our Christmas to be a lot of things," says McKinley. "Full of joy. Memories. Happiness. Above all, we want it to be about Jesus. What we don't want is stress. Or debt. Or feeling like we missed the moment. Advent Conspiracy was designed to help us all slow down and experience a Christmas worth remembering. But doing this means doing things a little differently. A little creatively. It means turning Christmas upside down."

The idea behind Advent Conspiracy is to make Christmas the revolutionary event it was meant to be, encouraging communities at Christmas to worship fully, spend less, give more, and love all. Churches take the season of Advent (the four weeks before Christmas) and do their best to take the focus off consumerism, be reminded of the real reason Jesus came to the world in flesh, and pool their resources (saved from not spending on meaningless gifts) to apply them to a meaningful cause.

Instead of giving Dad another useless tie, churches encouraged children to make a gift for Dad and put their money toward something more lasting—like potable water for children in need. Instead of an unwanted item for Mom, or a toy for Brother that will break in a week, kids write a card, paint a picture, or go on special family outings—and use the money saved to meet a real need.

What started out as a handful of churches has become a beautiful example of the unity God calls us to—1,700 churches in seventeen nations on four continents raising more than $2.5 million last year to meet serious needs around the world!

The idea challenged us here in Portland. We wondered if, as a group of churches, we could combine our efforts and give a collective gift back to the city that would express our love for Portland in a very tangible way. The idea came in the midst of the economic downturn. We knew the City of Portland was struggling to live within revenue projections *and* meet needs. So we did what we always do. We met with our city leaders, including Mayor Adams and County Commissioner Diane McKeel, and asked, "What's something that has to be cut from the budget that would meet people's needs?"

As in most major cities, there's a growing awareness of the serious issue of sex trafficking. At the time, Portland had no shelter for the victims, many of whom were teenagers. The city had hopes to build a facility, but they just couldn't find the funds. We put our heads together as the church. What if we joined with the city and county, along with social-service agencies, to help create such a shelter?

That first year, the churches pooled their resources and gave a gift to the city—$100,000 to be exact! They also mobilized volunteers. Together with Janus Youth Services, we were able to repurpose an existing shelter and create a safe place for seven victims. Not enough, but a start.

That was a few years ago. The momentum has grown since. And nothing is more fun than taking time every December as the body of Christ to come together and meet with city officials to ask what their most pressing needs are. I'm sure they love it, too!

Another expression of this unity—another beautiful story—is a movement started in Portland in 2008 called Seven. Initially launched by John Mark Comer at Bridgetown: A Jesus Church, the vision was simple—to gather for a week of prayer and fasting, asking the Lord to move in a fresh way in the city. The first year included a handful of churches. The next year, a few more. Now, seven years later, it has grown to include more than one hundred churches throughout the region—every size, shape, denomination, and background. They commit themselves to seven consecutive days of fasting and gather for evening prayer services in different locations throughout the city. No agenda. No speakers or bands. Just 10,000 joyful Christ-followers joining in simple worship and prayer, seeking the peace and presence of God on behalf of the city. (Jon Tyson from Trinity Grace in New York City leads a similar effort there called Citywide Worship.)

The unity of this gathering speaks volumes to me. I love seeing churches reach outside their own walls, but Seven is special because it focuses its prayer and fasting on the physical and spiritual needs of Portland.

Practically speaking, when we sacrifice for others, giving up something to fast and pray, we join with them in their need and celebrate with them when that need is filled. In this way, Seven helps us relate better to God so that we can relate better to our community.

Though we don't serve or pray or give for selfish reasons, when we do these things, we find our own lives changed and fulfilled as a result. We join with God in his work and, by his grace, reap the blessing of standing with him, of continuing on in loving service for others.

It's easy to be self-reflective as a Christian and focus only on my own needs or the needs of my family, but something happens when I spend time praying for my city. I become attached more intimately to it. I begin to care for it. And when our hearts move toward caring, it usually coincides with some kind of action.

A gathering like Seven reminds us that the gospel message itself is beautiful, because it teaches us truth about this world, about ourselves, and, most important, about the goodness of God. It has the power to incite and sustain change in our lives and in our communities. It extends past our immediate needs and unveils the needs of a world hungry for the abundance of God's love.

Are we serious about spiritual renewal in our cities across America? I believe if we are, then our intent will be evidenced by how much we pray and how united we stand as a church.

I know the typical Christian might be tempted to see prayer as kind of a given. "Oh, of course we pray," some might say. But I find too often prayer and other spiritual disciplines get glossed over too quickly. I can't emphasize enough how important prayer is as we seek to lead.

Leaders here in Portland, in our movement, try never to move forward with an initiative without first bathing the idea in prayer. Prayer is a theological hub for our community action. Prayer helps us assume a right posture of humility and obedience to God. When we make God central to our decision-making process, we invite his blessing and wisdom into our lives. By seeking God's will in our endeavors we open ourselves up to his direction. This requires patience, silence, the will to act when we receive peace about moving forward, and the humility and strength to hold back when we sense he is guiding us in a different direction.

Prayer also exposes our faults before God. It allows us to deal with our shortcomings. By simply asking God to help us promote unity in our neighborhood, we are actually admitting to God that we might be deficient in this area. This posture of humility gives

God free reign to guide and direct us, to teach and instruct us in an area where we've lagged.

Transparency before God tells him of our willingness to change. It shows our readiness to listen to his word and to obey it better each day. It can be scary at times to ask God to help us in a weak area, because chances are he'll use that opportunity to push us out of our comfort zones. But once we're out of our safe little church boats and walking on the waters of faith with him, we discover how we were made for so much more.

Spiritual renewal in our cities must always begin *in us*. We are often viewed as hypocritical beings, because we don't spend nearly enough time challenging and calling out our own brokenness, as individuals and as a Christian community. Even Jesus calls us out on it: "You hypocrite! First take care of the plank in your own eye before you start worrying about the speck in your neighbor's eye" (Matthew 7:5, my paraphrase).

It's pretty clear and obvious but, sadly, not what most folks see us doing. Seven is a great time for those of us in Portland to repent collectively of that often unintentional hypocrisy, not in a choreographed routine of false pretenses or thoughtless legalism, but genuinely giving us a chance to quietly reflect on the log in our own eye.

There's something dignified about humility. Why were people so drawn to the person of Jesus? Why are we drawn to leaders like Mother Teresa, who built no empire, encouraged no cult of personality? It's because they simply loved and served those in need.

Humility takes discipline and time. It demands an unflinching ability to look at ourselves in the mirror and admit when we've been wrong. Rather than creating a group of cringing, self-doubting men and women, this sort of honest humility and self-reflection brings hope and healing.

During the second year of Seven, I brought Sam Adams with me to one of the gatherings. We met at River West Church, a vibrant congregation in Lake Oswego led by Guy Gray. It was a drizzly Tuesday evening and getting dark as we arrived. There were 1,000 men and women there, praying and worshiping, overflowing the sanctuary. We slipped in and joined a small group of twenty-somethings fervently praying for God to work in our hearts, to change us and make us more like Christ as we seek to share the Good News and bless the city. Then it was time for me to go up on stage with Sam and ask him how we could pray for him and the city. Sam asked for prayer as he and the commissioners made the inevitable hard decisions at budget time. They knew the decisions they made affected people directly on the ground. He asked for prayer related to new efforts to combat human trafficking and also asked for prayer for our schools. Right then and there, Christopher Coffman, outreach pastor at River West, led us all in prayer—for Sam, for the commissioners, and for the issues Sam had raised.

After the gathering, I walked Sam out, back to his car. That's when he turned to me and said, "What just happened there? Where did all those people come from?"

Sam didn't know how to process 1,000 people, most under the age of forty, coming out on a rainy Tuesday evening to pray in unity for him and the city. And the reality is, I didn't know how to process it either. It was simple and beautiful and powerful.

Soul Homework

Psalm 133 says, "How wonderful and pleasant it is when brothers live together in harmony! For harmony is as precious as the anointing oil that was poured over Aaron's head, that ran down his beard and onto the border of his robe. Harmony is as refreshing as the dew from Mount Hermon that falls on the mountains of Zion. And there the Lord has pronounced his blessing, even life everlasting" (NLT).

Pretty clear! We all know it's wonderful and pleasant when we live together in harmony—in unity. The Psalmist uses two images: the precious anointing oil poured over the head and the refreshing dew on Mount Hermon.

Anointing oil is sacred and precious. It symbolizes the setting apart of the High Priest, Aaron in this case, for his role before God. And the dew up on the mountain, such a pleasant reprieve from the hot desert sun. It brings life. The Lord blesses and calls good this sort of harmony and even ties it to "life everlasting." We know it's our destiny to be one, eventually and forever. How sweet to experience some of it now! And why should we wait?

Both of these images may seem a little obscure to us, but we know it's good. Deep in our souls we know it's good when we're in harmony—one in spirit and purpose—with fellow believers in Jesus.

Harmony, above all, is rooted in selflessness. It is experienced as we put others above ourselves. Few practiced this more clearly than Dallas Willard.

John Ortberg's great book, *Soul Keeping*, provides a glimpse into the amazing life of Dallas Willard, a man who gently and gracefully walked through life in an unhurried way. He had an impact on people like few others have. For those of us seeking to be a part of all God is doing, here's some "soul homework" from Dallas:

If you want to really experience the flow of love as never before, the next time you are in a competitive situation, pray that the others around you will be more outstanding, more praised, and more used of God than yourself. Really pull for them and rejoice in their success. If Christians were universally to do this for each other, the earth would soon be filled with the knowledge of the glory of God.

Amen and well said! Yet what a challenge!

I believe I'm seeing that sort of self-sacrificing Christian solidarity in Portland already. Pastors consciously speaking well of one another. Genuine joy when other churches grow, even if their own is struggling to make ends meet. Excitement when a competing nonprofit discovers a better way to tackle an issue and a new source of funding.

This amazing love for each other not only puts us in a better place to serve the needs of the city, it better reflects the God we serve. It changes perceptions, tears down walls, reshapes stereotypes, and reflects the true beauty of the gospel.

Chapter Six

What Moves Us Will Move the World:

Unlikely Stories

I had always felt life first as a story; and if there is a story, there is a story-teller.

—G. K. Chesterton

The gospel message—at its core—is a story. A dramatic, grace-filled story. A true story of sacrifice, forgiveness, and reconciliation. Who doesn't like a good story? Who isn't moved by a beautiful story?

One of the reasons Christian influence and effectiveness have waned is that we've not always told our stories well. We've let lesser stories dominate and confuse us, and we've taken the greatest story ever told—of a creator who came to seek and save his creation, a love story really—and reduced it to platitudes that can fit on a bumper sticker.

As we seek to serve our communities and draw those we love and live with to Christ, telling a truer, better story is essential. "Truth" and "story" are not antithetical. Theology does matter. At the same time, Jesus modeled storytelling as one of the primary ways to express his timeless truth.

Some of the best ways we've seen our gospel movement progress in Portland has been related to how we've put a spotlight on the beautiful stories that have emerged from our partnership and service. The best way we've found to keep the movement going and keep it fresh and energized is to relentlessly look for and tell the stories of God at work through his people. Nothing models "best practice" better and inspires action than giving people a glimpse of how the Spirit is leading others in their efforts to reflect Jesus.

I spend a fair bit of my time traveling around the country talking about the "Portland Story." That's what I've ended up calling it, because it's really not a philosophy of ministry and it's certainly not a program I'm trying to sell. It's a beautiful story of God at work in some fresh ways through his people in a particular time and place.

Stories inspire people in a way that mere facts and figures can't. I could tell you that the dropout rate in the Portland public schools was more than 50 percent at one point and that Roosevelt High School was underperforming. I could maybe even show you some graphs and pie charts, but I wouldn't expect much of a response. Anyone who followed the news here knew that information, and still nothing much changed. Southlake got engaged because of a story. A story told by Wilson Smith after visiting the Roosevelt campus. He saw the need for himself, firsthand.

Steve Duin writes stories for a living. He's so good at it that he's been the top columnist at the *Oregonian* for years. Tough but fair-minded, you don't want to get on his bad side! Steve's storytelling ability was one of the key factors in the amazing outcomes at Roosevelt. Steve was a sportswriter for years before moving onto his three-times-per-week column that's the heart and soul of the paper (in my humble opinion). Steve can be relentless in his pursuit of a story, and in some ways he plays a prophetic role as the conscience of our city, using his gift of storytelling at times to shame us or to lift our vision of what could be. He came to that first remarkable makeover, where more than 1,000 people joined together to serve. Steve knew there was a story there, and it went way beyond mere numbers. He made it his mission to not let his readers forget Roosevelt.

Part of the story was the women's basketball team at Roosevelt. They had struggled for years. They lost far more games than they won and enjoyed virtually no fan support. Try twenty or so souls per game. In Steve's efforts to experience life at Roosevelt, he attended a game and sat in the empty bleachers. He knew sports' ability to shape the lives and hearts of young people, and his heart ached at the missed opportunities. The last game of the season was coming up, and as he wrote about the early stages of the renaissance of Roosevelt, he challenged his readers to join him for the last game. Kip, Wilson, Kristine, and other Southlake leaders grabbed hold of the story and helped pack the stands to overflowing. More than 1,000 crammed into the gym to cheer on the lady Roughriders. They lost the game but gained a family.

A story well told is a powerful thing.

———

A story well told is a powerful thing.

———

Sometimes the power of a story isn't in telling it but in listening to it. After the 2008 Festival and first CityServe effort, about half of the fifty largest and most influential churches in the Portland area were engaged. "All in" as I like to say. The others were in no way opposed; they just had a variety of other things vying for their attention. I never quit working on building relationships with the other twenty-five. I made a point of getting appointments to visit those that were at least open to meeting.

I remember the first time I met Chris. He's a vibrant young leader who guides the outreach efforts for a thriving church in the southern suburbs of Portland. He seemed a little wary. Polite, but a bit aloof. When we sat down, the first words out of my mouth were "I'd love to hear your story. What are you excited about? What do you see God doing here at your church?" He looked a little surprised. Wasn't I there to pitch him on some sort of project or event? Was there another Palau Festival coming up? No, I was genuinely curious to hear how God was working in his life and at his church. That threw him a bit, but as he began talking, things began to change. He warmed up and enthusiastically told me about a ministry the church had launched to reach out to mostly older folks living in two low-income hotels downtown. They'd begun serving communal meals regularly.

"Could I help you tell that story?" I asked. "Maybe other churches would want to join in? Could you folks use some help with this?"

That began a strong friendship that's thriving today. Four other churches are now helping lead this hotel ministry, and the previously less engaged congregation is now helping lead the way in the movement.

Sometimes listening to someone else's story and helping pass it along is the most important thing you can do.

Stories have power. They cast vision and push ideas forward. They allow us the ability to celebrate and accelerate existing work.

Here are just a few stories that have personally touched me through this unlikely journey in Portland.

Embrace Oregon: Loving Kids in Foster Care

Some stories take years to emerge and flourish. Like that of Luke and Jillana Goble. They love kids. Over the years, Luke and Jillana had undergone the training to become foster parents, and out of that experience they adopted a daughter. The countless hours spent at the Department of Human Services (DHS) office near their home had let them see firsthand the challenging environment faced by all involved: staff, caseworkers, foster families, birth parents, and of course the children themselves. Budget cuts over the years had left the office in a sad state and the staff juggling caseloads that at times were beyond their ability to cope.

The Gobles attend Imago Dei, which does a great job empowering their members to think and act creatively. They applied for a missional grant, and Jillana started a small effort to provide welcome boxes so that kids entering the system would have something to call their own as they started this challenging time. Something put together lovingly, by hand, to say "you are loved." Josh Butler, the outreach pastor at Imago Dei Community Church, emailed me and Ben Sand, an amazing leader who cofounded the Portland Leadership Foundation.

"I wonder if we could share the story of the needs of DHS and the foster care system with other churches?" he asked.

We began—as we've learned to do—by sitting down with the heads of the various DHS offices and simply sharing the Gobles' story. We ended our time with each of the offices by saying, "We love you and are so grateful for the way you serve our most vulnerable kids. Is there anything we can do to make your life easier? How can we help you succeed?"

I'll never forget the reaction on some of their faces. One woman began to cry and said, "No one has ever come in here asking how they can help. Everyone who comes in to see us is in crisis, angry, upset, or frustrated. If the media comes around, it's because something has gone horribly wrong despite our best efforts. But no one has ever come in to offer help."

They didn't know what to do with a group of local churches wanting to seek *their* peace and prosperity. Not surprisingly, after they heard the story of the Gobles, they had some great ideas of their own. Over the course of the next twelve months, Ben and his team at the PLF spearheaded the creation of what's now known as Embrace Oregon. They partnered with DHS to renovate six of the nine regional offices, turning them into more inviting and comfortable places for the kids who walked through their doors in the midst of crisis. In addition, dozens of churches gathered together to create and donate more than 7,000 welcome boxes for the kids served by DHS, many of whom are pulled from their homes in a rush, often in the middle of the night with no time to collect personal items. The boxes included toiletries, general necessities, a few small toys, and notes of encouragement. Several churches also gathered together to brainstorm other ideas to serve foster kids and foster parents. They came up with Foster Parents' Night Out, a once-a-month, DHS-approved, open-door program for foster parents to drop off their kids for a fun night out with new, safe faces in the community (all DHS-trained and approved helpers), while giving the parents a few hours to themselves. The churches also came up with the idea of office moms and dads—trained volunteers willing to give their time to look after kids and keep them company as they wait in the DHS offices. Just another opportunity to show we care and to seek shalom.

Ultimately, our goal is to help find more than eight hundred new foster parents—many of them from the Christian community—who are willing and able to take in the children who are still stuck in the system, finding them loving, caring homes while their complicated and painful situations are figured out. The power of a story.

Why did we do all this? Certainly in humble obedience to Christ's command to love our neighbors as ourselves—there is no question the children in the foster care system are our neighbors.

An improved foster care system helps everyone, just as the success of our school system helps all of us, as well as that of the kids and families in our community. Have you ever stopped to think about how all these things connect? Where do many of the kids come from who end up on the streets or are trafficked? Many are from the foster care system.

Humble service. Incredible influence.

Compassion Clinics

Another story that's spread across the metro area is that of the Compassion Clinics. Milan Homola is a humble and effective young guy who came from Minnesota to the Pacific Northwest to study at Multnomah. He's even more of a Timbers fan than I am, so you gotta love the guy. He eventually became copastor of a church in Gresham, east of Portland and a place of high need. As northeastern Portland has gentrified, much of the poverty has migrated to Gresham and East Multnomah County.

What began as a simple one-day effort by Clear Creek (Milan's church) to meet needs by offering free medical and dental care has grown and grown as the story spread. There are now fifteen one-day clinics across the metro area each year, providing one of the best practical ways for churches to collaborate to meet needs. One of the aspects I most love is the personal touch they give and the way they use the power of storytelling. A typical clinic works with about two hundred volunteers. Not because they need that many doctors or dentists, but because the goal is to try to have someone to personally connect with each guest if possible. Over lunch and as time is spent waiting for appointments to open up, volunteers share their own stories of struggle, pain, or redemption. Guests also share stories of courage or pain in the midst of the challenges that poverty and homelessness provide. And often, the conversation leads to the hope and confidence that comes from the presence of Christ. These clinics are about sharing stories along with pulling teeth.

City Bible Church and Their Rest Stop for Law Enforcement Officers

City Bible Church is a leading ministry in our city, with three church campuses and more than 5,000 people who worship together every weekend. They have not only been part of all the collaborative efforts (school partnerships, Compassion Clinics, Embrace Oregon);

they've also stepped up when it comes to serving law enforcement officers and first responders in our city.

Just recently, their leadership decided to repurpose a room on their main campus and turn it into a rest stop for police officers—a safe haven from the stresses of the job where they can take a break, write their reports, and breathe for a few minutes. It's like a luxury suite: television, kitchen, beautiful couches and furniture, even high-speed Internet. The officers have their own code, allowing them to come and go, day or night. As City Bible Church has served the officers, they've naturally built strong relationships of trust. And now, the police department knows where to turn when they need help. In fact, City Bible is now often asked to host some of the largest gatherings for law enforcement officers in the area.

Sonrise Church—A Place for Those in Recovery and Prisoner Reentry Programs

James Gleason, pastor of Sonrise Church in Hillsboro, Oregon, is another humble visionary. He and the church are tireless in their efforts to serve those leaving prison and trying to reenter society. It's a group with challenges, for sure. They include sex offenders and individuals in recovery from serious addiction. Many of them want to come to church but must be careful who they are around. The church had a solution—create a separate service just for these folks.

More than one hundred individuals attend this service weekly, and many have come to faith in Jesus and are baptized every year. This humble service has led to James serving on several task forces with the mayor of Hillsboro, dreaming of the future of this city of 100,000 people.

11:45 and the Gang Violence Prevention Effort in Northeast Portland

As in most major metropolitan areas, gang activity challenges some of our neighborhoods. When a spate of shootings rocked the city in 2012, Mayor Adams knew exactly what to do. He worked to convene the churches in the area to discuss what could be done. What emerged was an initiative called 11:45. Under the leadership of amazing pastors like Mark Strong and George Merriwether, 11:45 sent out teams of residents, young and old, to walk hot spots identified by the police. The agenda was simple—just be a quiet presence, make friends, smile, shake hands, get to know people. Hundreds of people canvassed the area. And the result? Crime dropped dramatically. Gang activity was pushed out. The parks and streets became safe again. Shalom. Peace. Prosperity.

A New Story in Your Neighborhood

Stories shape our lives and can change the lives of others. Stories have the capacity to equip and inspire in phenomenal ways.

———

Stories have the capacity to equip
and inspire in phenomenal ways.

———

Ask yourself, "What sort of fresh story could we tell in our neighborhood? In our church?" You may not be in a situation where hundreds of churches in your city are collaborating on a large scale.

But perhaps there's a church nearby that could benefit from your support, encouragement, and friendship. What if you were to sit down with their leaders—or encourage your pastor to do it—and ask them how you could serve them? Is there something you could do together in your neighborhood? Is there something that could further the influence and impact of each of your congregations and help meet the real needs in your community? This can often start by simply celebrating the great work already taking place in both of your churches. Share stories. Pray for one another. Praise the Lord for what's already being done. There are almost always existing efforts underway. We just don't take the time to listen and find out what they are.

Personally, I've found that relentlessly telling the good stories of God at work is the single best way to inspire and cast fresh vision and effort. Seminars and formal training are great and most definitely needed, but we've found that putting forward the best practices and great examples that are already evident in the city naturally unleashes all sorts of new energy. Start by celebrating what's already working, and build from there.

In Portland, we send out simple emails every month to more than 6,000 friends throughout the city. The only focus—to tell five stories of God at work through local churches, groups of churches, and nonprofit organizations. By selecting the right stories, you're modeling, in a very practical way, what you see as valuable and fitting for the community.

Here's a simple exercise. I encourage every church to do it. You can even do it within your own family or small group. Have a three-to-four-minute show and tell. Allow someone from within your congregation to share how they are living out their faith in a practical way. I guarantee the time will bless others and challenge many to think differently about how they are reaching out.

The stories I could share would go on for pages. How the churches of Portland have joined together, sought out the needs of the city, have served in humility, shared the gospel, and given generously. God has done so much in this most unlikely city of Portland. Whether it's the work of Door to Grace and their efforts to love and serve the victims of sex trafficking, Embrace Oregon and the huge steps they have taken with the church to work on the foster care system, or Second Home and all they do to find homes for homeless high school students in the Beaverton School District. Each one is helping tell a better story—a more fulfilling, hopeful, beautiful, grace-filled story—based on the Good News of Jesus Christ. A story grounded in unity, partnership, humility, and service.

Building greater church-to-church collaboration not only encourages the churches involved, but it blesses the community by making things easier for city leaders and school officials. They know where to go, who to ask for help, and what to expect. They don't have to organize a team, because you've already done it. Our city leaders—mayors, school superintendents, etc.—don't have the time, energy, or expertise to build collaboration among churches. That's our job. And it's a huge practical blessing to them. It's what Jesus himself prayed for, remember?

Chapter Seven

Building the Foundation:

An Unlikely Movement

Seek the peace and prosperity of the city to which I have carried you . . . pray to the Lord for it, because if it prospers, you too will prosper.

—Jeremiah 29:7

People have often asked me, "How did this movement in Portland begin?" It's the right question, in one way. If we love our city, town, or neighborhood, we want to see God work there. And why not learn all we can from what he's doing elsewhere? But there's a hidden danger. There's no surefire formula or one-size-fits-all program to be followed.

This understandable question can miss the point. We never set out to establish a movement in Portland. That wasn't on our minds at all, at least not at first. We set out to remain obedient to Christ's call to proclaim his message, live in unity as his followers, and love our neighbors. What a huge relief that is! If it had depended on us, it would have been bound to fail. "Fixing Portland" wasn't our goal either. What a burden that would be. The issues and problems that arise in Portland and in your community have developed over generations and have deep roots. Thinking we can fix every problem and meet every need is a recipe for burnout, frustration, and anxiety.

———

Thinking we can fix every problem
and meet every need is a recipe for
burnout, frustration, and anxiety.

———

Our "movement" in Portland isn't our movement at all; it belongs to Jesus. There's never been a more powerful movement in the history of the world than the gospel movement Jesus began. Just think of it. Abolition? Hugely important. It was led by William Wilberforce and many others throughout Great Britain—many driven by their deep Christian faith. A movement with a defined season. What about the labor movement? The civil rights movement? Prohibition? All vital in their seasons, and all certainly moved millions to action. But nothing comes close to the long-term impact of this gospel movement. Its breadth is astounding—historically, linguistically, geographically, culturally.

Another way to describe the gospel movement, of course, is to talk of it the way Jesus did—as the kingdom of God. What is the kingdom of God? The simplest way I've heard it described was by my friend John Ortberg. He put it in the context of Jesus's prayer in Matthew 6:9–10: "Our Father, which art in heaven, Hallowed be thy name. Thy kingdom come, thy will be done in earth, as it is in heaven" (KJV).

Simply put, the kingdom of God, his rule and reign, is where God's will is done on earth as it is in heaven.

God's will is not as mysterious as we make it out to be. We know it's not God's will that extreme poverty, child abuse, human trafficking, hunger, homelessness, and many other social ills exist. Far from it! Our efforts in the name of Christ to love and serve our neighbors is kingdom-building work. It goes hand in hand with sharing the Good News. After all, it's not God's will that any should perish, but that all should come to repentance (2 Peter 3:9). It's God's will that we obey his great commission to go into the entire world and share the Good News. The kingdom of God is visible now, and yet there is a not-yet aspect to it, as the full expression and fulfillment will not come until the return of Christ.

Jesus talked about the kingdom in many different ways. In Matthew 13:31–32, Jesus said, "The kingdom of heaven is like a mustard seed, which a man took and planted in his field. Though it is the smallest of all seeds, yet when it grows, it is the largest of garden plants and becomes a tree, so that the birds come and perch in its branches."

When a mustard seed starts out, it's small and seemingly insignificant. It goes into the ground and dies, yet springs forth in new life and ends up blessing the broader community. It's "like yeast that a woman took and mixed into about sixty pounds of flour until it worked all through the dough" (Matthew 13:33). Slowly, invisibly, it works and grows, and in the end, it changes the nature of the entire lump of dough.

Recognizing that the seemingly small efforts we all make as followers of Christ contribute to the movement in our city is cause for rejoicing. It all counts, even when it may not be on the front page of the paper. So in a very real way, every single believer, church, and

Let's let our actions *and* our words preach, and let's allow our hearts to be informed by our heads and seek efficiency and goodness in not only our message but also our methods.

The needs around you and me shine with opportunity—an opportunity for you and me to bloom where we're planted.

Chapter Nine

An Oregonian Reflection on a Talking, Walking Gospel:

Unlikely Outcomes

Out of one hundred men, one will read the Bible, the other ninety-nine will read the Christian.

—Dwight L. Moody

The gospel is always about relationships. With God and with others. This unlikely movement winds its way through history one life at a time. It's only through relationships that individual Christians and the church can hope for any true and lasting impact. In any relationship, humility is the key to trust, effectiveness, and lasting influence. For those of us who long to see kingdom impact in our cities and lives, and to see folks come to faith in Christ, humility must mark our endeavors. It must lead us into common-ground relationships where we serve with and not simply for others. Where we cultivate deep friendships among our brothers and sisters in

Christ, and where we seek the peace and prosperity of our communities. Where we're passionate about humbly serving and sharing the life-transforming message of Jesus that has changed our lives.

This ongoing Portland journey has reminded me of the simplicity of it all. Love God and love your neighbor as much as you love yourself. Our culture values innovation and thrives on the economy of ideas—and I love new ideas. But when we begin to value our innovative ideas over our devotion to God and care for others, we stray from the Way.

I wonder what it would look like if we really obeyed Jesus's command to follow him in all our endeavors. When we find the strength to bend our knees and see the world through *his* eyes and do what *he* commanded, our efforts will bear fruit and bear witness to the kingdom of God.

When we find the strength to bend our knees and see the world through *his* eyes and do what *he* commanded, our efforts will bear fruit and bear witness to the kingdom of God.

Our Portland story moves forward with no one really owning it. Hundreds of leaders and thousands of individuals have kept the gospel front and center and have provided fresh vision and creativity in the way CityServe Portland expresses God's love in practical ways. And it's not just a spark—flashing quickly, finding moderate success, and burning out. Rather, it's a fire, ignited by the one person that matters—that person who is beyond this world—that person who continues to lead us all in his Way.

Reflect with me now on a few perspective changes crucial to the gospel movement.

Reconciling Relationships

The movement Jesus started reconciles all relationships. With God and with others. "God was in Christ, reconciling the world to himself. . . . And he gave us the wonderful message of reconciliation" (2 Corinthians 5:18 NLT). And all ministry begins first with deep and honest relationships. The movement in Portland began not because we targeted our mayor, but because we approached him and asked how we could work with him to build a better Portland.

We found common ground in the needs of our community.

We laid our differences aside and cared for one another.

We worked for local change, and in the process we grew close, established a strong trust, and accomplished great things within the body of Christ and with those who, in the past, wouldn't have wanted to identify with the church.

Now the fruit of these relationships has taken root. It was the same relationship of trust we built with Portland public school superintendent Carole Smith that we build with the various Department of Human Services offices. Christ-followers, motivated by their love for God and their love for people, expressing a genuine and unaffected sense of gratitude and respect. Conversations that began with "thank you for serving our community and making it better" before asking, "How can we help?" It's the same simple question Jesus asked 2,000 years ago: "What do you want me to do for you?"

We don't need to pretend to be the best at helping. We don't need to impress anyone with our skills or abilities to solve every problem. In fact, those we seek to serve with will often be more skilled than we are. They've lived their situation, and they may have a clear vision of what needs to be done. Our job, then, is to humbly ask, "Can I make your life easier?"

My friend Rick McKinley always reminds me, "We're not here to fix Portland. That would just be overly tiresome. We are here to display the love of God."

The greatest way to soften hearts and open doors for the gospel is to be in genuine relationship with people.

Sometimes folks will ask, "How do you measure the impact of this work?" A fair question, no doubt, and one that's not always easy to answer. I could say, "Two hundred fifty-three public schools across sixteen different school districts now have some level of partnership with a local church, and we aim to establish four hundred such partnerships by 2018." But of course that doesn't answer the question of what those partnerships have accomplished.

I could point to churches that would say they're baptizing more people than ever before, or to thriving churches in Portland's urban core that weren't there ten years ago.

I could say, "Well, Roosevelt High School's on-time graduation rate has climbed fifteen percent in the past three years, and they've doubled the number of students." But someone might still reply, "Can you demonstrate how the Southlake partnership directly contributed to those gains?" And on and on it could go.

I'm not saying we shouldn't measure (to some degree), or in other ways demonstrate, the impact of what we're doing. We should be good stewards of our time and resources. We should challenge ourselves to work as effectively as we can and spend money in ways that make a difference. Sharing good stories of impact furthers the movement, but it's a slippery slope if we're serving to be noticed and praised, or to gain influence. Going down that road can lead to either pride or discouragement, depending on what we're measuring, or tempt us to shade the truth or hide the results that aren't as shiny. We serve and share the Good News out of genuine love and obedience whether or not we see immediate results, even though sometimes the impact can't be felt for years to come.

Jesus didn't seem to worry too much about measuring what he did. He didn't seem to have a clearly discernible strategy, by our standards. He did invest in a small band of leaders and empower them for ministry. In general, though, he walked from town to town, and whoever happened to show up—friends tagging along with other friends, or people just randomly wandering by—heard him tell his stories and witnessed him heal those in need. I'm trying hard to learn this kingdom strategy—this dependence on the Spirit of Jesus for guidance and power and boldness.

I want to fully trust God with the results of what I do or what God seems to be doing in Portland and elsewhere. It's *his* kingdom and *his* Spirit empowering thousands of ordinary folks who are tucked into big companies like Nike and Intel, working as baristas at Starbucks, teaching fourth grade at William Walker Elementary, writing for the *Oregonian*, or blogging, or even preaching on Sunday mornings. He's the one motivating people into loving and caring about the real-life situations of neighbors, children, and folks in their own communities.

When I think about the 2,000-year history of the kingdom Jesus inaugurated in a fresh way on the day of Pentecost in Jerusalem, it is cause for rejoicing and taking a deep breath. A breath of gratitude that the progress of the kingdom doesn't ultimately depend on me or you, or your pastor, or Luis Palau, or even the church in the good ol' US of A. We've been well trained by our culture to measure everything, to constantly compare ourselves to others, and now, thanks to social media, to countless folks we will never even meet! They always seem smarter, better-looking, richer, more sophisticated, better educated, and probably even more humble and godly! It's great news that this amazing gospel movement is not of our making; and while we're privileged to answer the call and empowered to contribute to it, its ultimate progress is in God's capable hands.

———

It's great news that this amazing gospel movement is not of our own making; and while we're privileged to answer the call and empowered to contribute to it, its ultimate progress is in God's capable hands.

———

The gospel moves forward entirely on relationships and is best measured by the depth of love we have for God, among ourselves, and for those who seem far away. If people saw that kind of love and forgiveness lived out, then a great deal of the questions could be laid to rest. The flare of anger that comes when people hear the word "Christian" would fade. More would be drawn to Jesus.

We would learn to truly rejoice when we hear of good things happening to fellow brothers and sisters in Christ: the raise they got, the church down the street that's growing, the flourishing marriage, or the kids that graduated on time from college. We would be able to care and sympathize with the struggles that come our way. If we can learn to be faithful in the smallest things, the smallest relationships, we'll see amazing things happen. Not because we're personally changing everything, but because we're getting out of the way and allowing folks to see the beauty of this Jesus movement across the lives of tens of thousands in our city, in all of our churches.

How exactly did we keep this in focus? How did we focus on relationships and, thus, speak the language of God to our entire city?

We found common ground in the needs of our community.

Finding common ground is key in *any* relationship! If Sam and I didn't think we possessed any common ground, then there would be no relationship, no friendship. It's crazy (and discouraging) to me to see how little common ground we perceive and pursue even within our Christian community!

I was a religious studies major at Wheaton College and loved both my historical theology and church history classes. It helped me grasp why there are so many thousands of denominations, where they came from, why the splits happened. It helped me to see the incredible potential for unity that can still exist, the core of shared belief that can be built on, within the diversity of language, style, structure, culture, and interpretation of Scripture. I'm not saying these differences are irrelevant, that theology doesn't matter, or that you shouldn't care what denomination (or nondenomination) you're part of. I *am* saying, however, that we need to work hard for biblical unity and to find common ground wherever we can. After all, Jesus prayed we would.

When there's common ground, we can care enough and respect each other enough to actually engage on the topics we agree on, and we can trust each other enough to argue and talk through our differences. We need to fight the temptation to separate from each other when we disagree. I've had such a joyful experience finding common ground with those who, in the past, would have crossed the street to avoid talking to an evangelical like me.

We laid our differences aside and cared for one another.

How we treat each other within the body of Christ is another key to any movement's progress. Do I see other churches in the same light I see my own—just as vital to kingdom progress? Do I listen to and value church leaders from other cultures? Do smaller churches matter as much as larger ones? Do I see other ministries as the competition if they're in the same space and meeting the same needs? Church history is full of bad examples, and those who've been hurt by us in some way love to throw that in our faces. We can't change past church history, but we can write a bit of it ourselves, in our own communities and neighborhoods.

We worked for local change and, in the process, grew close, establishing strong trust and accomplishing great things together.

I'm so inspired by those here in Portland who have really embraced their neighborhoods and towns. I love the way Dave Brewer and AllOne Community have embraced North Portland and are always dreaming and conspiring to make it a better place: better schools, better opportunities for jobs, better neighborhood associations and PTAs, better local nonprofits, and better churches. It's the same with Rich Jones and the Hillsboro Ministerial Association. With groups of pastors praying in North Clackamas and Canby and Oregon City. In Northeast Portland with the Albina Ministerial Alliance. We would all love to see a revival of historic proportions sweep across this country and the world. It's happened before, in pockets and seasons, and I've prayed for it and read about it, I'm guessing, as you have. I don't know if it's something we can pray into reality or not. I do know, however, that nothing and no one can stop me from serving joyfully in my local church, sharing the gospel with my neighbor, and volunteering in my local school to read to a third-grader.

As we've seen God inspire several hundred pastors and church leaders with a vision for the gospel to flourish in both word and deed, we've seen some amazing things happen. Most of them have happened slowly and have begun to produce the kind of fruit that makes me smile and think about the kingdom. It's that invisible strand of yeast working heart to heart, church by church, and it's working in a way that no one person can take credit for. It's that tiny mustard seed, dying and rotting in the ground, and then living and flourishing and bringing life to all that is around it.

The same sorts of kingdom efforts are also happening in many other cities.

Getting to know peers in cities across the country—Chip Sweeney in Atlanta, Rebecca Walls in Dallas, Sam Williams in San Diego, Billy Thrall in Phoenix, Ray Williams in Little Rock, Jeff Kreiser in Sacramento, Jon Tyson and Mac Pier in New York City, Jon Talbert in San Jose, Chris Gough in Seattle, among so many others—has filled me with joy and gratitude. If this is a movement of God's Spirit, we shouldn't be surprised that similar efforts are taking place all across the country and the world. They're all very unique, but they share characteristics and a DNA that can be traced back to two things: the same Spirit of Jesus and strong local relationships.

Originality, Simplicity, and Naked Bike Riders

I've said many times that I absolutely love living in the Portland area. Over the years, people have sometimes expressed surprise as to why the Luis Palau Association is based here.

"Aren't you guys primarily effective in Latin America? Isn't your dad Argentine? Why do you live there?"

Up until ten years ago my only answer was that my mom is a native Oregonian and that it made sense for us to live there since Dad was traveling so much and Mom's family was there. Now, however, I see things a little differently.

I'm convinced God has us here for a reason, that while I'd really like to believe we (meaning the hundreds of churches and non-profits and thousands of believers) are making a difference in Portland—changing Portland, if you will—I *know* that Portland has changed us. I think it should always be that way.

We impact our culture and are in turn changed by it. I don't mean being conformed to the image (or pattern) of the world, as the apostle Paul warned, being watered down or adopting anti-kingdom values. I mean looking for the image of God even in those who might seem to be far from him at the moment. I'm not sure we'll ever get the balance right, but I think that we can rejoice and trust that God has us where he wants us, and that it's *his* movement, and that we can find joy and inspiration in our unique location.

What makes Portland *Portland*? What makes your city or town unique?

Portland's a place that values diversity and freedom of expression. It has a thriving indie music scene, and bands like the Shins, Decemberists, and Modest Mouse make their way to this great place where they can be mostly left alone. It's a place that feels

European in its love for both kinds of football. It's a place that thinks deeply about the environment and how not to lose the natural beauty we've been blessed with. Yes, there's a lot of rain, or at least many months of cloud cover, but that's what feeds our rivers and lakes and caps Mount Hood year-round. We have easy access to high deserts, rain forests, large rivers, the Pacific Ocean, and beaches that belong to the public.

We're also a place where churches get along pretty well, partly since no one church or denomination rules the roost. We're blessed with a number of churches with several thousand attendees every week, but no behemoth of 10,000-plus. I think that reality has produced a healthy humility in the area—a sense that we have to work together if we want to bless and impact our region. And that's a good thing.

That's our story. But what's yours? What makes your hometown, well, *home*? I think that when you feel at home, with a special sense of place, it's easier to dig in and fight for the local scene. We're such a transient society. I get that. But just because we move around doesn't mean we can't be present right where we are. Let's stop waiting for the next big move and dig in for the next big movement.

The Unlikely Nature of the Gospel

Unlikely is Christ's modus operandi! He is always turning cultural expectations on their heads. It seems unlikely that such a movement would flourish in very progressive, unchurched Portland, yet it is right in line with how Christ works. When he walked the earth, he confronted the status quo of religious leaders, drawing uneducated fishermen, tax collectors, and women to his side. What an unlikely start to an unlikely movement!

I like the word "unlikely"—"not likely to happen." What could be more unlikely than the gospel? How unlikely that the God of the universe would choose one particular tribe of people to initially reveal himself. How unlikely that he would reveal himself most fully by choosing to become human in the person of his son, Jesus, the Messiah. And, what's more, in so doing he would be born of a teenage peasant girl, in a small, insignificant town. No one noticed it—except the livestock and the shepherds—until Jesus was an adult. It was only after the resurrection, in hindsight, that even his close followers finally comprehended the significance of the moment.

How unlikely that this Messiah would suffer a horrible, but common, death by crucifixion, only for his followers to pronounce his resurrection from the dead? How unlikely that to be part of the Jesus movement we just need to recognize our need and humbly choose to repent from our rebellious ways and follow him?

It doesn't feel so unlikely to some of us who've grown up believing it. But of course to many Americans, and others in the West, it's unlikely to the point of madness—nothing more than an embarrassing historic relic to radically redefine into oblivion.

God has always chosen the foolish things of this world to shame the wise. God values faith and humility while the world values self-dependency and visible success and pride. We feel comfortable around people who live at peace with themselves, who do not need to push themselves forward. Yet Jesus railed against the religious hypocrites—those men and women who shared a sense of spiritual pride. If you have no sense of your own need, there is nothing God can do for you.

I love the simple parable of the righteous religious Pharisee who prays and thanks God that he's not a sinner like the tax collector he sees, while that same man is humbly begging God for mercy. It's against all common sense and human nature to be made right with God by simply admitting our intrinsic need for him. Not works, just need. Not even great faith. Just faith, even as small as a mustard seed. There's nothing we can do to earn his love and trust and salvation. Now that's an unlikely story.

I rejoice in the unlikely nature of the Good News. How dynamic to look upon Portland—a most unlikely place for a gospel movement to take root, for the kingdom to be displayed—and witness the continued cultural transformation of lives through simple acts of service.

So, to answer all those who ask "Why Portland?" I say this: because leaders were humble and recognized our need.

If we didn't know we needed each other, then we wouldn't seek unity. If we didn't recognize our general lack with regard to what it takes to make a dynamic impact, then we wouldn't seek God in a regular week of prayer and fasting called Seven. Since we realize that it's God's movement and not ours, freedom comes in refreshing waves. And that freedom allows us to find new friends in unlikely places, to joyfully seek kingdom enterprises together. Since we know we can't lose, we can love and work with people very different from us, joyfully sharing the Good News in the process.

Since we know we can't lose, we can love and work with people very different from us, joyfully sharing the Good News in the process.

And that, dear friends, is the gospel message: a bit unorthodox, a bit uncalculated, and totally unlikely.

Grateful

For several years, I hesitated to write this book, because I felt it wasn't fully my story to tell, but rather the collective story of many thousands of Jesus-followers from across the Portland metro area, some known and many quietly and humbly serving with no thought of anyone else being aware of their efforts. I pray that everyone whose efforts continue to contribute to this Portland story will feel a certain sense of satisfaction, as what they do inspires others to "go and do likewise."

Dangerous as it is to start mentioning leaders by name, I am grateful for pastors who have walked together in this effort: Rick McKinley, John Mark Comer, Mark Strong, Will Hardy, T. Allen Bethel, Tim Osborn, James Gleason, Gabe Kolstad, James Martin, Christopher Coffman, Randy Remington, Tim Smith, Dave Teixeira, Jason Curtis, Milan Homola, Marc Estes . . . (I shouldn't have started!).

I'm grateful for city leaders like Portland mayors Tom Potter, Sam Adams, and Charlie Hales, as well as city commissioners like Amanda Fritz and Nick Fish who risked their reputations by willingly joining hands with us before they knew us well. For school superintendents like Jeff Rose and Carole Smith, and principals like Charlene Williams, who likewise took a step of faith to trust that good would come from unlikely partnerships.

Nonprofit leaders like Bill Russell, Gary Tribbett, and Marshall Snider have put up with my trying to tell their stories and cheer on their efforts. Ben Sand, Jillana Goble, and Anthony Jordan from the Portland Leadership Foundation and Embrace Oregon have been a huge inspiration to me and to leaders in other cities.

Cindy Kirk, Larry Whittlesey, and Brianna Woods have humbly served the overall CityServe efforts in Portland, picking up the pieces of my countless half-formed ideas and turned them into something beautiful.

And of course, those who helped make this book possible: Matt Yates, Jessica Wong, Jay Fordice, and Tim Willard. Without your guidance and support, this book would still be stuck in my head. Thank you.

Notes

Chapter 2: The Only Time We've Got:
An Unlikely Context

1. Go here for more: http://www.pbs.org/wgbh/pages/frontline/shows/religion/why/appeal.html.

2. http://www.earlychristianwritings.com/tertullian.html.

3. Marcianus Aristides, *The Apology of Aristides*, argument 15, to Caesar Titus Hadrianus Antoninus, A.D. 125. See: http://www.newadvent.org/fathers/1012.htm.

4. Eusebius, *Ecclesiastical History* 9.8.13–14.

5. Abraham Lincoln, Second Inaugural Address, March 4, 1865.

Chapter 5: The Powerful Role of Unity:
An Unlikely Prerequisite

1. Orthodox Church of America (paraphrased).

Chapter 7: Building the Foundation:
An Unlikely Movement

1. Henry Blackaby, *Experiencing God*, 130.

Chapter 8: Get Local, Dig Deep:
An Unlikely Mission

1. Joshua Butler, *Why We Love Our City*.http://joshuaryanbutler.com/2014/08/why-love-our-city/.

2. Electronic source: http://www.oregonlive.com/news/oregonian/steve_duin/index.ssf/2014/04/steve_duin_changing_the_world.html.

3. Electronic source: http://parishcollective.org/about/.

4. See the 2011 *Christianity Today* interview with Jon Tyson.

5. Ibid.

6. Brian Fikkert, *When Helping Hurts*, 74.

7. For more on doing good service, see "When Service Is Selfish," *Leadership Journal*, July 2014.

About the Author

Kevin Palau is the son of international evangelist Luis Palau. He joined the Luis Palau Association in 1985 and began directing the day-to-day operation of the ministry in the late 1990s. Under his leadership, LPA has produced some of the largest Christian events ever staged, drawing large crowds on nearly every continent. In 1997, Kevin helped develop the Next Generation Alliance (NGA), LPA's partnership to encourage and equip a new generation of evangelists, which now includes more than five hundred partner evangelists. In 2008, Kevin pioneered the Festival 2.0 model, which integrated a major community service initiative called CityServe. Kevin is also the founding editor of GospelMovements.org and is a regular speaker at national conferences such as Catalyst, Movement Day, and Q Ideas. He holds a degree in religious studies from Wheaton College and lives in Beaverton, Oregon, with his wife, Michelle, and their three children.